1992

LIEUTENANT
SCHMIDT

The author, Viktor Shklovsky, Pyotr Neznamov, Osip Brik, Sergei Tretyakov and Vladimir Mayakovsky. Sokolniki, 1925

ЛЕЙТЕНАНТ ШМИДТ

Boris Pasternak

LIEUTENANT SCHMIDT

Translated into
English verse by
RICHARD CHAPPELL

Bilingual edition

SB
SPENSER BOOKS
LONDON
1992

Spenser Books, 2nd Floor, 6 Spenser Road,
London SE24 0NR

Distributed by Central Books, 99 Wallis Road,
London E9 5LN

British Library Cataloguing-in-Publication Data.
A catalogue record for this book is available from
the British Library.

ISBN 0-9513843-2-5

Set by R & D Graphics
17 Willow Lane, Mitcham, Surrey, CR4 4NX

Printed by Abacus Printing Co Limited London EC1R 0BN

CONTENTS

Duty to the Future   vii

Lieutenant Schmidt
(in Russian and English)

    First Part   3

    Second Part   33

    Third Part   59

Notes   92

Bibliography   97

Verse-Forms   98

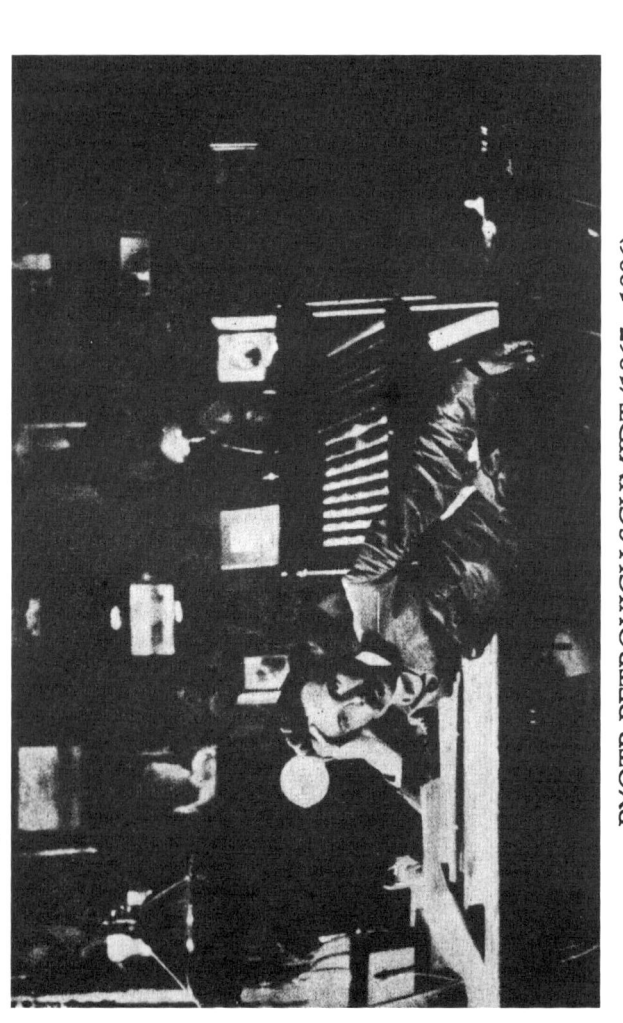

PYOTR PETROVICH SCHMIDT (1867 - 1906)
In his study at Sevastopol.

'Orpheus burst nationality, or he
extends it to such breadth and width
that everyone (bygone and being) is
included.'

TSVETAEVA

'....and there shall be no more death,
neither sorrow nor crying, neither shall
there be any more pain for the former things
are passed away.'

Rev. 21:4

'All the world must suffer a big jolt.
There will be such a game that the
ungodly will be thrown off their seats,
and the downtrodden will rise.'

MÜNZER

DUTY TO THE FUTURE

Boris Leonidovich Pasternak (1890-1960), the Russian poet
known especially for his novel, *Doctor Zhivago*, initially
studied music but switched to philosophy, his first poetry
only being written in 1912. With 'My Sister - Life', a cycle of
lyrics composed in the revolutionary days of mid-1917, he
was thrust to the forefront of modern Russian poetry and
was quickly considered the heir to the traditions of
Lermontov, Tyuchev and Blok as well as an artist uniquely
attuned to the flux and spirit of the revolutionary era. As the
son of an impressionist painter and a musician, his
upbringing gave him an all-round artistic sensibility while,
being from a materially unprivileged background, his art
was to be fashioned by common human perception. In 1937
he was to write to the Union of Soviet Writers which had
challenged his commitment to the people:

'...the fact is that individuality without the people is
transparent and that any emanation of it, the authorship

and the merit of its driving force, harks back to it - the people. The people is the master craftsman (carpenter or lathe operator) and you the artist are the raw material.'

Though he continued to produce lyric poetry almost to his death, throughout his life he was striving to write convincingly in prose, a form he felt more appropriate to the concerns of the present century. With this in mind, he wrote three epic poems between 1923 and 1927: 'The High Malady', 'The Year Nineteen-Five' and 'Lieutenant Schmidt', each of which reflect aspects of Russia's revolutionary experience. Upon the appearance of the last two works in a joint volume in 1927, Pasternak explained: 'the epic is implicit in our age and, accordingly, in the book 'The Year Nineteen-Five', I am moving from lyrical modes of thought to epic-writing, very hard though this is.' His son, Evgeny Pasternak, has since observed that epic-writing was in turn a self-imposed training-ground for narrative prose work.

'The Year Nineteen-Five' is a selective survey of events of the first Russian revolution and, despite the author's misgivings over the poem's artistic validity, retains remarkable lyric, epic and visual power. 'Lieutenant Schmidt', however, ventures into fields later to be more fully investigated in *Doctor Zhivago*. The individual's moral duty to society and history, the interaction of public and private responsibilities and the feasibility of non-violence as a tool of social advance are questions that already crystallise in Pasternak's extended verse treatment of the uprising of sailors, soldiers and workers at Sevastopol in November 1905 and the role of its leader, Pyotr Petrovich Schmidt. 'Lieutenant Schmidt' thus takes its place alongside *Doctor Zhivago* as Pasternak's most accomplished and universal work. Its creation, moreover, required a rigorous study of documents, memoirs, personal correspondence and court transcripts so that, at the high points of historical drama, Pasternak stayed loyal to the known facts and eschewed romanticising and stagecraft.

On March 17 1926, the author received a letter from his father, Leonid Osipovich, in Berlin, reporting that the poet, Rainer Maria Rilke, Pasternak's childhood hero, had discovered the poetry of the young Russian and spoken ecstatically of it. At the same time, Pasternak had just come across Marina Tsvetaeva's long work 'Poem of the End', 'that endless sequence of poignant lyrics of Michaelangelesque breadth and Tolstoyan quietude' as he put it enthusiastically to its author. Marina Tsvetaeva, in 1905 a student and admirer of Schmidt, was to maintain an intimate correspondence with Pasternak as he wrote 'Schmidt' whose first part was originally prefaced by an acrostic dedication to her. These two unexpected experiences proved to be catalysts to Pasternak's artistic energy which he felt had ebbed irreversibly since his collection 'Theme and Variations' of 1918.

The First Part of 'Lieutenant Schmidt' was started early in March 1926 and submitted for publication to *Novy Mir* on May 18. Prompted in part by Tsvetaeva's doubts about the intrusion of unheroic aspects of Schmidt's personality, Pasternak was to excise a number of passages from his character's letters in this part when the whole poem came out in book form the following year. The chapters of the Second Part were composed from September 1926 to January 1927 and the Third Part followed between February and April 1927. The effort of creating 'Lieutenant Schmidt' caused enormous intellectual and emotional stress to Pasternak who at times was working on the poem for approaching twenty-four hours day while at others, as at Christmas 1926, suddenly finding his strength wholly drained.

In writing his revolutionary poems, Pasternak assumed his readers' familiarity with the historical events dealt with, particularly as in 1925 a wealth of material was issued to commemorate the revolution's twentieth anniversary. In an article on translating Shakespeare's history plays, the author noted that as with ancient heroic poetry, Greek tragedies based on the myths and religious mystery plays, epic historical works of literature presume the plot to be common knowledge to the audience or reader. 'Art starts at the secondary level' as he expressed it.

Pyotr Petrovich Schmidt was born on February 5 1867 in Odessa, the only son of a naval officer who eventually attained admiral's rank. With his father often away at sea, his mother dominated his early upbringing to be followed by his older sister, Marusya, upon her death when Pyotr was in his early teens. Unlike her mother, however, Marusya had an erratic character and mystical leanings while Pyotr, though nervous, impressionable and of weak health was more intellectually and morally disciplined. He attended Berdyansk gymnasium and entered the St. Petersburg Naval Academy in 1884. Promoted to the officer corps in 1886, he passed out two years later to serve with the Imperial Baltic and, then, Pacific Fleets. In 1893 he married, exchanged into the reserve and joined the merchant navy as a captain, sailing chiefly to the Middle East, East Africa and Brazil. According to personal reminiscences, he was highly respected by crews for his navigational and technical expertise and, class origin and rank notwithstanding, an exemplary attitude towards his men. With the outbreak of the Russo-Japanese War he was called up first to serve in the roads off Sevastopol and then, on appeal, to join the fleet auxiliary 'Irtysh'. Following that vessel's grounding mishap in the Suez Canal he was posted to a torpedo-boat squadron as second lieutenant at Ismail on the Danube and it was from there in July 1905 that he absented himself without leave to attend to a family crisis in the Crimea. Changing trains at Kiev, he went to the races where he first saw Zinaida Riesberg, the encounter that Pasternak took as the starting-point for his poem.

Although up till then, Schmidt had not been active in any political organisation, he did hold definite liberal populist views, read widely, (also writing poetry and playing the cello) his ideas being largely formed by the

Narodnik writers Mikhailovsky and Shelgunov, who were highly influential among the young intelligentsia of the 1880s. He also took part in discussion - group activity and is known to have produced lectures on the land question and the oppression of women under capitalism.

He personally grew up with a progressive, if exalted, view of women of which his wife does not appear to have been worthy. Thus his marriage collapsed and, taking custody of his one son, devoted himself to his education. Young Evgenii was to remain with him until the day his father was invited to take charge of the Sevastopol uprising, as recounted by Pasternak in the third chapter of the Second Part of the poem. Schmidt's friendship with Zinaida Riesberg which Pasternak brings in as a counterpoint to the drama of the uprising and its aftermath was commonly thought to have given Schmidt the moral stimulus and self-confidence for his courageous leadership of the sailors, soldiers and proletarians of Sevastopol.

In the companion poem 'The Year Nineteen-Five', Pasternak highlights key events of the year like Bloody Sunday in January, the Lodz insurrection and the 'Potyomkin' mutiny in June and the Moscow rising in December. The Sevastopol rising with which 'Lieutenant Schmidt' is exclusively concerned took place between the October all-Russian political strike and the Moscow rising, lasting from November 11 to 15. But Vice-Admiral Chukhnin, charged with the repression of the revolutionaries at Sevastopol, admitted to the Tsar on the 17th that 'the military storm has abated but not so the revolutionary one'.

Traditions from the 'Potyomkin' days had lived on in Sevastopol for Chukhnin's punitive measures had little impact on insurgent morale only buttressing mutinous moods in the fleet so that the October strike inspired in Sevastopol a period of vast street demonstrations, with sailors as well as infantrymen acting not just as participants but as speakers too.

The rallies swelled and moved to the square between the naval barracks and the quarters of the Brest regiment. Since service personnel were not allowed to attend workers' assemblies, the workers inundated the soldiers' gatherings which grew to tens of thousands. The idea of joint action took root and the advanced companies elected their deputies to the Soviet. The sailors, who formed the core of the uprising, with all their greater resourcefulness and self-reliance, encountered however deeper antagonism from the closed upper-class caste of officers than did troops in the army where half the officers had come through the ranks. Hence the hostility to Schmidt from his former academy colleagues. Moreover, the humiliation of the command in the operations against Japan had demolished any respect the ratings might still have nurtured towards their captains and admirals.

Pasternak's poem has been rightly described by Christopher Barnes in his *Boris Pasternak: a literary biography*. as 'an amazing compendium of experiment in the field of strophics, metre and rhyme' adding that 'there is nothing to match this spectacular prosodic laboratory elsewhere in Pasternak's oeuvre'. But the poet dissociated himself from aesthetic indulgence: in 1931 he wrote to the Union of Soviet Writers in the discussion 'On Political Lyric Poetry', '...talking about the craft of poetry-writing is to talk about self-destruction... you have to bear in mind that you need to take risks as nothing on earth exists without taking risks.'

Pasternak, whose instinct for rhythm, tune and form was always consonant with the spirit and content of his verse and born of his musical training, found it hard to avoid being sidetracked from epic narrative in 'Lieutenant Schmidt' by the emotions of his hero and drawn into lyric digressions. In addition, the Third Part of the poem was composed after news reached him of Rilke's death which was a body blow to the author's morale and doubtless enhanced the tragic impact of its closing chapters. In commemorating Verlaine's centenary in 1944. Pasternak had remarked that , as a true lyricist, the French poet had left 'a vivid account of things experienced and things seen', as a realist in the same spirit as Rilke, Blok, Ibsen and Chekhov, 'Verlaine reaches naturalism without seeking to charm and without stirring from the spot'. An echo of this approach is to be found in lyric passages throughout 'Schmidt'. 'Realism is ... that crucial measure of the admixture of artistic detail which neither the general rules of aesthetics nor the listeners or viewers of his time dictate to the artist' Pasternak wrote on Chopin. Naturalism and objectivity have more valid vitality than romantic art which 'has at its command stilted pathos, pseudo-profundity and simulated sensitivity.' Chopin is, like Tolstoy a great realist, whose art is thoroughly genuine not by distinctness from its rivals but by its affinity with the nature from which it is created. Referring to Pushkin's 'Eugene Onegin', Pasternak elaborated on objectivity in art as follows: 'Subjectively, the poem is what the poet has just written. Objectively it is what he is now reading, or correcting in the galley proofs, something written by a being greater than himself.' The autonomy of Pushkin's heroine, Tatyana, from the poet's control is recalled in 'Schmidt' by the presentation of Zinaida Riesberg in the Third Part where her quest for the imprisoned hero is written with Pushkinian or Tolstoyan detachment and thus, true pathos.

The character of Pyotr Schmidt has been seen as a precursor of Yury Zhivago, a messianic, 'enemy of bloodshed', thereby ascribing to the poem a Tolstoyan moral doctrine. But Tolstoy, as Lenin was to observe, also reflected the stifled hatreds and aspirations of the common people and, with it, the unpreparedness for revolutionary struggle which contributed to 1905's failure. The role of Schmidt, the radical middle-class intellectual non-party man springs from the last act of 1880s' populism and forms the overture to 1917 'on the very border of two historic instants'.

Schmidt led proletarians to fight for democratic and economic rights such as the bourgeoisie and liberal nobility were unable to achieve: the political crux of 1905.

In the First Part of the poem the author borrows an image from Tsvetaeva's 'Poem of the End' in implying a parallel between the genesis of Christianity and revolutionary progress. Engels had drawn a comparison between the early Christians fighting slavery and the workers' movement rising in defence of its rights. But Pasternak's image 'from circus churchwards, games - hierarchy' acquires an added undertone appearing as it did in 1927 and the days of nascent Stalinism.

In 1956 Pasternak reflected on the mass upsurge of 1917: 'People who had passed through the harsh school of the outrages showered upon the poverty-stricken by power and wealth, understood the revolution as the explosion of their own wrath, their lethal retribution for the prolonged and ever-protracted mocking torment.' And of Lenin, twelve years on from Pyotr Schmidt, he wrote 'Unwavering and with the ardour of genius, assumed responsibility for such blood and demolition such as the world had not yet seen and would not flinch at roaring a war-cry to the people, appealing to their most recondite yearnings, thus permitting the sea to rage and the hurricane to rampage only at his behest.' Furthermore in 1958 in a letter to Vyacheslav Ivanov, he wrote 'art in itself is a striving only justifiable in relation to the future.'

Not by chance then that 'Lieutenant Schmidt', watershed and masterpiece in the work of Boris Leonidovich Pasternak, pledges that the human weal and thereby art itself shall be rediscovered and reshaped in every age to come.

R.C.

ЧАСТЬ ПЕРВАЯ

1

Поля и даль распластывались эллипсом.
Шелка зонтов дышали жаждой грома.
Палящий день бездонным небом целился
В трибуны скакового ипподрома.

Народ потел, как хлебный квас на леднике,
Привороженный таяньем дистанций.
Крутясь в смерче копыт и наголенников,
Как масло били лошади пространство.

А позади размерно бьющим веяньем
Какого-то подземного начала
Военный год взвивался за жокеями
И лошадьми и спицами качалок.

О чем бы ни шептались, что бы не́ пили,
Он рос кругом и полз по переходам,
И вмешивался в разговор, и пепельной
Щепоткою примешивался к водам.

Всё кончилось. Настала ночь. По Киеву
Пронесся мрак, швыряя ставень в ставень.
И хлынул дождь. И как во дни Батыевы,
Ушедший день стал странно стародавен.

FIRST PART

1

The fields' horizon oval-spread is flattened lying,
While thunder-thirsting sunshade silks breathe gasping.
A blazing day is training its unfathomed skyline
Upon the racecourse grandstand at that Derby.

The folk perspired like kvass kept ice-cold in a cupboard.
So spellbound by the melting mist of distance.
The horses churned and whipped up spaces into butter,
And swirled amidst a whirl of hooves and shinpads.

Yet in the rear to drifts of even beating pulses
Of some deep subterranean beginning
Behind the jockeys' backs that year of war was gusting
Up wicker rocking-chairs to horses' whinnies.

Whatever lingered whispering, in whatever drinks,
Around it grew across the walkways crawling.
It chipped straight into conversations: in a pinch
Of cinders dropped and mingled in the waters.

It's all now over. Night's arrived. Through Kiev a rampage
Of racing clouds and casement banging casement.
The rain teemed down. And just as back in Batu Khan's age,
The last departed day seemed strangely ancient.

«Я вам писать осмеливаюсь. Надо ли
Напоминать? Я тот моряк на дерби.
Вы мне тогда одну загадку задали.
А впрочем, после, после. Время терпит.

Когда я увидал вас... Но до этого
Я как-то жил и вдруг забыл об этом,
И разом начал взглядом вас преследовать,
И потерял в толпе за турникетом.

Когда прошел столбняк моей бестактности,
Я спохватился, что не знаю, кто вы.
Дальнейшее известно. Трудно стакнуться,
Чтоб встретиться столь баснословно снова.

Вы вдумались ли только в то, какое здесь
Раздолье вере! — Оскорбиться взглядом,
Пропасть в толпе, случиться ночью в поезде,
Одернуть зонт и очутиться рядом!»

'I'm plucking courage up. It's all quite needless
Remembering. I'm that racegoer, the sailor.
Back there you landed me one frightful teaser.
That later, later on though. Time is patient.

When first I saw you there ... Before that meeting I
Somehow survived although all lay forgotten,
I gave pursuit at once, upon you keeping eye,
The crowdbound past the turnstile went and lost you.

But once my awkward tongue-tied bug had vanished,
It struck me that I didn't know that girl there.
What followed you well know. So hard it is to manage
Things for us to meet again, fantastically, covertly.

Have you yet pondered simply what free rein and range
For trust lies in all this? In umbrage at my staring,
You plunged lost in the crowd, by night to chance upon a
    train
And furl umbrella, wow, you're my compartment sharing!'

Над морем бурный рубчик
Рубиновой зари.
А утро так пустынно,
Что в тишине, граничащей
С утратой смысла, слышно,
Как, что-то силясь вытащить,
Гремит багром пучина
И шарит солнце по́ дну,
И щупает багром.

И вот в клоаке водной
Отыскан диск всевидящий.
А Севастополь спит еще,
И утро так пустынно,
Кругом такая тишь,
Что на вопрос пучины, —
Откуда этот гром,
В ответ пустые пристани:
От плеска волн по диску,
От пихт, от их неистовства,
От стука сонных лиственниц
О черепицу крыш.

Известно ли, как влюбчиво
Бездомное пространство?
Какое море ревности
К тому, кто одинок!
Как, по извечной странности
Родимый дух почувствовав,
Летит в окошко пустошь,
Как гость на огонек.
Известно ль, как навязчива
Доверчивость деревьев.

To sea a stormy weal
Of ruby-tinted dawn.
The morning's so deserted,
That, silence-soaked, seems quite to match
All loss of sense, yet's heard then,
As if some fish trying hard to catch,
The depths its gaffs clang searching
While sunlight gropes the seabed
To probe out with its gaff.

And down a watery sewer
That disc all-seeing's asked for.
But Sevastopol's still asleep,
And morning's so deserted.
Around lies such a hush
That to the questioning depths:
From where comes that dull thunder,
Those empty quaysides answer:
From waves that splash the disc,
From fir-trees, from their fury,
From sleepy larches tapping
The rooftop tiles they brush.

Do you not know how amorous are
Those voids of homelessness?
And in what seas of jealousy
Swims one who;s all alone?
How long estranged so endlessly
Yet sensed a kindred soul
May fly the wastelands through the window
Like guests into a fold?
You don't know just how tightly cling
The trusting trunks of trees?

Как, в жажде настоящего,
Ночная тишина,
Порвавши с ветром с вечера,
Порывом одиночества
Влетает, как налетчица,
К незнающему сна?
За неименьем лучшего
Он ей в герои прочится.
Известно ли, как влюбчива
Тоска земного дна?

Заре, корягам якорным,
Волнам и расстояньям
Кого-то надо выделить,
Спасти и отстоять.
По счастью, утром ранним
В одноэтажном флигеле
Не спит за перепиской
Таинственный моряк.

Всю ночь он пишет глупости,
Вздремнет — и скок с дивана.
Бежит в воде похлюпаться
И снова на диван.
Потоки света рушатся,
Урчат ночные ванны,
Найдет волна кликушества
Он сызнова под кран.

How in such thirst for truthful things,
The nighttime's silent peace
Will leave the breeze since eventide
Amid a fit of loneliness
To raid as in a robbery
The one who knows no sleep?
For lack of something better yet
He's made himself her hero.
Do you not know how amorous is
Our earth's deep bowels' spleen?

First light amid snagged anchor-chains,
The waves and far horizons
Must single out a living soul
To save and so defend.
What fortune, bright and early
In some low single-storied wing,
Mysteriously, quite sleeplessly,
A sailor sits with pen.

All night he's writing silly poems,
A nap – from bed then leaping,
To water rushing, dowse it down,
Then straight back into bed.
Streams of light are crashing round,
The nights' drained bathtubs gurgle.
The wave finds him hysteria-bound,
Beneath that tap again.

«Давайте, посчитаемся.
Едва сюда я прибыл,
Я всё со дня приезда
Вношу для вас в реестр,
И вам всю душу выболтал
Без страха, как на таинстве,
Но в этом мало лестного,
И тут великий риск.

Опасность увеличится
С теченьем дней дождливых.
Моя словоохотливость
Заметно возрастет.
Боюсь, не отпугнет ли вас
Тогда моя болтливость?
Вы отмолчитесь, скрытчица,
Я ж выболтаюсь вдрызг.

. . . .

Вы скажете — ребячество.
Но близятся событья.
А ну как в их разгаре
Я скроюсь с ваших глаз?
Едва ль они насытятся
Одной живою тварью:
Ваш образ тоже спрячется,
Мне будет не до вас.
Я оглушусь их грохотом
И вряд ли уцелею.
Я прокачусь их эхом,
А эхо длится миг.
И вот я с просьбой крохотной:
Ввиду моей затеи
Нам с вами надо б съехаться
До них и ради них».

'Come on, let's get these matters straight.
I've only just arrived here,
Right from the day I first checked in
I'll book you on my list,
My inmost soul I had to blurt,
No qualms as if confessing,
Though in this lies few flattering words,
In that's the greatest risk.

The danger looms apace just when
Pour down dark days of showers.
My self, my own loquaciousness
Will mount up by the hour.
I'm fearful lest my rambling chat
Will scare you well away now.
While you, your thoughts keep secret, sphinx,
I'll blurt my whole lot out.

. . . .

You'll say: dear me, what childishness.
Events are drawing close though.
So how can I amid their fever
Stay hidden from your gaze,
It'll scarcely be well satisfied
With just one living creature:
You face will also lie concealed,
For you I was not made.
In thunderous rolls I'm by them deafened
And barely stay uninjured.
To ride out to their echo.
One trice that echo fades.
Yet here I am with petty plea:
In view of my commitment
I need to take a trip with you
Before them, for their sake.'

4

Октябрь. Кольцо забастовок.
О ветер! О ада исчадье!
И моря, и грузов, и клади
Летящие пряди.
О буря брошюр и листовок!
О слякоть! О темень! О зовы
Сирен, и замки и засовы
В начале шестого.

От тюрем — к брошюрам и бурям.
О ночи! О вольные речи!
И залпам навстречу — увечья
Отвесные свечи!

О кладбище в день погребенья!
И в лад лейтенантовой клятве
Заплаканных взглядов и платьев
Кивки и объятья!
О лестницы в крепе! О пенье!
И хором в ответ незнакомцу
Стотысячной бронзой о бронзу:
Клянитесь! Клянемся!

О вихрь, обрывающий фразы,
Как клены и вязы! О ветер,
Щадящий из связей на свете
Одни междометья!
Ты носишь бушующей гладью:
«Потомства и памяти ради
Ни пяди обратно! Клянитесь!»
«Клянемся. Ни пяди!»

4

October, Strikebound and beleagured.
O gale force! O hell's fiendish ardour!
Where flutter spun strands from the harbour,
Seaborne shipments and cargoes.
O sea-squall of pamphlets and leaflets!
O quagmires! O murk! O implorings
Of sirens and latches and doorkeys
On the sixth in the morning.

From prisons to pamphlets and tempests.
O nights! O sweet freedom's proud ranting!
Maimed limp up confronting the salvoes
Like sheer standing candles!

O cemetery's moment of mourning!
With lieutenant's pledge's stern cadence
Sob nods of consent and embraces
From dresses and gazes!
O crêpe-shrouded stairways! O chorus!
To the stranger, in answer declaring
Hundred-thousand-strong bronzes all blaring:
'Then swear it! We swear it!'

O whirlwind, you, twisting tornado,
Snap phrases like maple- and elm-trunks
Worldwide of all ties you're protection
To mere interjections!
You waft on a raging smooth surface:
'In posterity's name we're bequeathing:
Not one inch to yield! So swear it!'
'We do. No inch yielding!'

Постойте! Куда вы? Читать? Не дотолчетесь!
Всё сперлось в беспорядке за фортами, и земля,
Ничего не боясь, ни о чем не заботясь,
Парит растрепой по ветру, как бог пошлет, крыля.
Еще вчерашней ночью гуляющих заботил
Ежевечерний очерк севастопольских валов,
И воронье редутов из вереницы метел
В полете превращалось в стаю песьих голов.

Теперь на подъездах расклеен оттиск
Сырого манифеста. Ничего не боясь,
Ни о чем не заботясь, обкладывает подпись
Подклейстеренным пластырем следы недавних язв.
Даровать населенью незыблемые основы
Гражданской свободы. Установить, чтоб никакой...
И, зыбким киселем заслякотив засовы,
На подлинном собственной его величества рукой.

Хотя еще октябрь, за дряблой дрожью ветел
Уже набрякли сумерки хандрою ноября.
Виной ли манифест, иль дождик разохотил, —
Саперы месят слякоть, и гуляют егеря.
Дан в Петергофе. Дата. Куда? Свои! Не бойтесь!
В порту торговом давка. Солдаты, босяки.
Ничего не боясь, ни о чем не заботясь,
Висят замки в отеках картофельной муки.

Hey, stop! Where are you going? Ye'll find it if ye seek it.
All's in disorder, jam-packed tight behind the forts,
What, afraid? Not at all, no command's to be heeded,
At God's behest the new-fledged land, dishevelled, wind-filled, soars.
Yet on that eve night's strollers on parade are harassed
By Sevastopol's ramparts' twilit outline sketch,
Crow-crowds arrayed in lines are swept clean from the bastions
To flight at once fast wheeling, in herds of cur-like heads.

All over gaunt forecourts are pasted up offprints
Of that moist manifesto. What, afraid? Not at all.
No command's to be heeded. His signature's blotted
With plaster daubed in glue round scars of recent sores.
Hereby granting the populace firm bulwarks unshaking
Of each citizen's freedom. Vouchsafing no power in the land.
And here jammed doorbolts stuck beneath blancmange still
     quaky,
On that authentic text, by autocratic hand.

Though still October lingers, white willows' withered shivers
Hide half-light that's plumped down to bring November's sulks.
To blame the manifesto or just the whim of drizzle, –
Chasseurs stroll round at ease as sappers sweep up sludge.
Sent from Peterhof, what's the dateline? Come on, lads! No
     retreating!
A crush down at the docks. Both tramps and soldiers march.
What, afraid? Not at all, no command's to be heeded,
Locks dangle loose in blisters of potato starch.

6

Три градуса выше нуля.
Продрогшая земля.
Промозглое облако во́ сто голов
Сечет крупой подошвы стволов,
И лоском олова берясь
На градоносном бризе,
Трепещет листьев неприязнь
К прикосновенью слизи.
И голая ненависть листьев и лоз
Краснеет до корней волос.
Не надо. Наземь. Руки врозь!
Готово. Началось.

Айва, антоновка, кизил,
И море Черное вблизи:
Ращенье гор, и переворот,
И в уши и за уши, изо рта в рот.
Ушаты холода. Куски
Гребнистой, ослепленно скотской
В волненьи глотающей волны, как клецки,
Сквозной, ристалищной тоски.

Аго́ния осени. Антагонизм
Пехоты и морских дивизий
И агитаторша-девица
С жаргоном из аптек и больниц.
И каторжность миссии: переорать
(Борьба, борьбы, борьбе, борьбою,
Пролетарьят, пролетарьят)
Иронию и соль прибоя,
Родящую мятеж в ушах
В семидесяти падежах.
И радость жертвовать собою,
И — случая слепой каприз.

To zero three degrees.
The chilled earth's set to freeze.
A hundred heads loom from a cloud that's dank and dull
Which with snow-dust is whipping round lank trunks,
And, taking on a leaden sheen,
In hail-filled breaths there dithers
The known hostility of leaves
In filth and muck to slither.
That naked hate of leaves and plants
Their hair to roots fast blushes, reddens.
You mustn't. Lie down. Arms apart!
It's started. So get ready.

The cornels, antonovkas, quince
Close by the sea's Black title glint
High raising peaks to overthrow,
All ears or earmarked, throat to throat.
From ear-pinched pitchers flow. With blows
From bestial blinding summits
You gulp down choppy waves like dumplings,
O stabbing angst of hippodromes.

Here's autumn's death agony. Infantry hordes
Antagonise marine invaders
Just as a maiden-agitator
Spouts forth jargon from chemists' and wards.
And that mission's ordeal: those parrying bawls
(The fight, for fight, in fight, by fighting,
O workers, workers, come ye forth)
All ears to muting inciting
With irony and salt-soaked spray
Declined into the seventieth case.
In self-sacrifice they're all delighting
And too in that blind whim of fate.

Одышливость тысяч в бушлатах по-флотски,
Толпою в волненьи глотающих клецки
Немыслимых слов с окончаньем на изм,
Нерусских на слух и неслыханных в жизни
(А разве слова на казенном карнизе
Казармы, а разве морские бои,
А признанные отчизной слои —
Свои?!)
И упоенье героини,
Летящей из времен над синей
Толпою, — головою вниз,
По переменной атмосфере
Доверия и недоверья
В иронию соленых брызг.

О государства истукан,
Свободы вечное преддверье!
Из клеток крадутся века,
По колизею бродят звери,
И проповедника рука
Бесстрашно крестит клеть сырую,
Пантеру верой дрессируя,
И вечно делается шаг
От римских цирков к римской церкви,
И мы живем по той же мерке,
Мы, люди катакомб и шахт.

In naval-style pea-jackets out-of-breath thousands
Of gulpers of dumplings in choppy crowds run,
Inconceivable words terminating in -ism,
Unrussian in sound and in life still unwritten,
(Surely not the same words cornice-etched so official
Upon barrack walls, nor battleship guns,
But the fatherland's dear gallant sons –
    That us?!)
While now that heroine in rapture
Swooping from the times at once to capture
The sea-blue throng – her head hung low,
Across the air's charged current racing
With trust and distrust alternating
To parody the brine-sprayed foam.

O graven image of the state,
Eternal ante-room to freedom!
From cages steals out every age,
Wild beasts roam round the Colosseum,
And preacher's hand intrepid raised
Shall christen cage-bars' pit-dripped dampness,
And tame with faith, house-train that panther,
Thus evermore a trail is blazed
From circus churchward, games – hierarchy,
And still we live by that same yardstick,
We, folk of catacombs, coal-faced.

7

Вдруг кто-то закричал: пехота!
Настал волненья апогей.
Амуниционный шорох роты
Командой грохнулся: к ноге!
В ушах шатался шаг шоссейный
И вздрагивал, и замирал.
По строю с капитаном Штейном
Прохаживался адмирал.

«Я б ждать не стал, чтоб чирей вызрел.
Я б гнал и шпарил по пятам.
Предлогов тьма. Случайный выстрел,
И — дело в шляпе, капитан».
«Parlez plus bas, — заметил сухо
Другой. — Притом я не оглох,
Подумайте, какого слуха
Коснуться может диалог».

Шагах в восьми от адмирала,
Щетинясь гранями штыков,
Молодцевато замирала
Шеренга рослых моряков.
И вот, едва ушей отряда
Достиг шутливый разговор,
Как грянуло два длинных кряду
Нежданных выстрела в упор.

'Look, infantry!' chance cries re-echo.
Alarm its apogee had reached.
Some company's buzz from dumps and depots
An 'order arms!' command now screamed.
Along the main road steps heard staggering
First faltered, haltingly to die.
Then, promenading past, the admiral
Cruised line abreast with Captain Stein.

'I'd rather not let this boil fester.
Hot on their heels, then down I'll crack.
A host of pretexts. Fired in error.
Then, certain, safely in the bag.'
'Parlez plus bas,' here dryly noted
The other one. 'I'm not yet deaf.
Remember everything we've spoken
All ears around will fast detect.'

Adrift in ribbons, dressed overall
Eight steps away, a line of chins
Half-turned and verst-long, eyes the strollers
Those sailors' gazes drink them in.
And scarcely had that glib discussion
Reached the naval unit's ears
When comes the crack of two shots running
Point-blank to catch them unawares.

Всё заслонилось передрягой.
Изгладилось, как, побелев,
«Ты прав!» — вскричал матрос с «Варяга»,
Георгиевский кавалер.
Как, дважды приложась с колена, —
Шварк об землю ружье, и вмиг
Привстал, и, точно куртка тлела,
Стал рвать душивший воротник.
И слышал: одного смертельно,
И знал — другого наповал,
И рвал гайтан, и тискал тельник,
И ребер сдерживал обвал.

А уж перекликались с плацем
Дивизии. Уже копной
Ползли и начинали стлаться
Сигналы мачты позывной.
И вдруг зашевелилось море.
Взвились эскадры языки
И дернулись в переговоре
Береговые маяки.

«Ведь ты — не разобрав, без злобы?
Ты стой на том и будешь цел».
— «Нет, вашество, белить не пробуй,
Я вздраве наводил прицел».
«Тогда», — и вдруг застряло слово —
Кругом, что мог окинуть глаз:
«Ты сам пропал и арестован»,
Восстанья присказка вилась.

All's overshadowed by the impasse.
All's blotted out, when cried 'You're right!'
A white-faced rating from the *Varyag*.
St George's decorated knight.
As twice he fired, to one knee dropping,
Then flung his rifle on the ground,
Sprang up, tore off his choking collar
As if his smouldering smock smelt foul.
He heard: for one that shot was deathly,
And knew the next one's lot was prompt.
He ripped the braid and gripped the medal,
An avalanche of ribs he blocked.

Between parade-ground and divisions
Flew warm exchanges. Start to loom
Terse call-signs from the mastheads signalled
Which crawl and drift in tufted stooks.
The sea abruptly started budging.
The squadron's tongues spun up and rose,
Towards negotiations nudging
The beacons ranged along the coast.

'Just claim you're mad, no motivation,
Stick to that tale and you'll be safe'.
'On no, your what's-it, no point feigning.
I all too sanely trained the aim.'
'Okay, then', words his throat congested –
As everywhere eyes stared around:
'You've had it now, yes, you're arrested',
The rising's flourishing lines unwound.

8

«Вообрази, чем отвратительней
Действительность, тем письма глаже.
Я это проверил на «Трех Святителях»,
Где третий день содержусь под стражей.

Покамест мне бояться нечего,
Да и — неробкого десятка.
Прими нелепость происшедшего
Без горького осадка.

И так как держать меня ровно не за что,
То и покончим с этим делом.
Вот как спастись от мыслей, лезущих
Без отступа по суткам целым?

Припомнишь мать, и опять безоглядочно
Жизнь пролетает в караване
Изголодавшихся и радужных
Надежд и разочарований.

Оглянешься — картина целостней.
Чем больше было с нею розни,
Чем чаще думалось: что делать с ней? —
Тем и ее ответ серьезней.

И снова я в морском училище.
О, прочь отсюда, на минуту
Вздохнувши мерзости бессилящей!
Дивлюсь, как цел ушел оттуда.

Ведь это там, на дне военщины,
Навек ребенку в сердце вкован
Облитый мукой облик женщины
В руках поклонников Баркова.

'Imagine as reality gets more foul
The letters that I write grow calmer.
I proved that when held in the *Three Patriarchs'* bowels,
For two days held there incommunicado.

Yet meanwhile I have nothing left to fear,
For after all I'm not a type so craven
To disavow that happening all so queer
With no sour rancour's taste left.

So why detain me for precisely naught,
He may as well have done with this indictment.
But how can I be spared those scurrying thoughts
Without a respite, daily, nightly?

Recall our mother, life's swift convoys fly
Once more all hindsight scrupulously avoiding
To cloud the famine and the rainbow light
Of gaudy hopes and disappointments.

You'll look round: the picture is more blunt.
But as the strife and discord sharpens
The more you wonder, what is then to be done?
Then ever sterner grows the answer.

Again I'm back inside the naval college
O, for one minute, to escape it!
For after air so vile and spirit-rotting
To get out sane, it's quite amazing.

Well, there it was when shipwrecked on cadetship
Were forged into my heart so child-like
A woman's features, pain-drenched and tormented
Culled direct from some Barkov admirer.

И вновь я болен ей, и ратую
Один, как перст, средь мракобесья,
Как мальчиком в восьмидесятые.
Ты помнишь эту глушь репрессий?

А помнишь, я приехал мичманом
К вам нá лето, на перегибе
От перечитанного к личному, —
Еще мне предрекали гибель?

Тебе пришлось отца задабривать.
Ему, контр-адмиралу, чуден
Остался мой уход ... на фабрику
Сельскохозяйственных орудий.

Взгляни ж теперь, порою выводов
При свете сбывшихся иллюзий
На невидаль того периода,
На брата в выпачканной блузе».

By her afflicted, I just keep on crusading,
A lonely finger midst benightment,
Or like some reckless youngster of the eighties
Repression's backwoods still to remind you.

Do you recall how, when I'd got my warrant
I'd come for summer, on my passage
To active officer from just a well-drilled scholar
But was my doom at that stage presaged?

And you had to keep our father happy
For him resigning was ridiculous ...
An admiral's son ,move to a factory
That builds and deals in farm equipment.

So look, in this hour for conclusions
By that light so darkly smothered
At such a spell of wild illusions
And at this soiled blouse of your brother.'

Окрестности и крепость,
Затянутые репсом,
Терялись в ливне обложном,
Как под дорожным кожаном.
Отеки водянки
Грязнили горизонт,
Суда на стоянке
И гарнизон.
С утра тянулись семьями
Мещане по шоссе
Различных орьентаций,
Со странностями всеми,
В ландо, на тарантасе,
В повальном бегстве все.

У города со вторника
Утроилось лицо:
Он стал гнездом затворников,
Вояк и беглецов.
Пред этим, в понедельник,
В обеденный гудок
Обезголосел эллинг
И обезлюдел док.
Развертывались порознь,
Сошлись невпроворот
За слесарно-сборочной,
У выходных ворот.

Солдатки и служанки
Исчезли с мостовых
В вихрях «Варшавянки»
И мастеровых.
Влились в тупик казармы
И — вон из тупика,
Клубясь от солидарности
Брестского полка.

The strongpoints and the outskirts'
Cords overcast in clouds
Were lost beneath those showers
In sailors' capes spine-bound,
The drab horizon spatters
Its dirty dropsied warts
That garrison's barracks
And ships in port.
In families, petty-bourgeois
Stretched roadbound from first light
With sundry orientation
And all their quaint demureness:
Their tarantass betakes them,
Dr landau, to massed flight.

The city which since Tuesday
Has not one face but three.
Safe nestles shy reclusives
Plus pugs and refugees.
Before that on the Monday
At lunchtime's siren stroke
The slipway roof fell dumbstruck
And basins drained of folk.
All singly ranged and disparate
That bumper crop elates
Assembly men and fitters
Around the exit gates.

Maidservants, wives and girlfriends
Fast vanished from the streets
Mid 'Varshavyanka's' whirlwinds
And labourers' swirling feet.
The barracks merged blind-alleyed
Then – clean from that dead end,
They're buoyed, supported, rallied
By Brest's foot regiment.

Тогда, и тем решительней,
Чем шире рос поток,
Встревоженные жители
Пустились наутек.
Но железнодорожники
Часам уже к пяти
Заставили порожними
Составами пути.
Дорогой, огибавшей
Военный порт, с утра
Катились экипажи,
Мелькали кучера.
Безмолвствуя, потерянно
Струями вис рассвет,
Толстый, как материя,
Как бисерный кисет.

Деревья всех рисунков
Сгибались в три дуги
Под ранцами и сумками,
Сумрака и мги.
Вуали паутиной
Топырились по ртам.
Столбы, скача под шины,
Несли ко всем чертям.
Майорши, офицерши
Запахивали плащ.
Вдогонку им, как шершень,
Свистел шоссейный хрящ.
Вставали кипарисы;
Кивали, подходя;
Росли, чтоб испариться
В кисее дождя.

With ever more unflagging
And broader surging floods,
These townsfolk stressed and anxious
Lost tails and heels to dust.
But gangs of striking railmen
Made sure by five o' clock
That tracks were barricaded
By empty rolling stock.
While by the road wide looping
Around the naval port
On carriages and coupés
Swift coachmen urged their horse.
In silence and quite feckless
The daybreak hung in streams,
So thick and coarsely textured,
Just like a pouch for beads.

The trees all sketched in pastels
Stooped low in threefold arcs,
Beneath the bags and satchels
Formed misty films of dark.
Fine veils like webs of spiders
Twitched bristling round pursed traps.
Poles galloped under tyre-treads
To wipe them off the map.
The officers' and majors'
Staid ladies wrapped their cloaks
As hornet-like there chased them
That hissing gravelled road.
Up rose a grove of cypress
Which first drew close then bowed:
It loomed, in vapour rising,
In rain-spun muslin shrouds.

ЧАСТЬ ВТОРАЯ

1

Вырываясь с моря, из-за почты,
Ветер прет на ощупь, как слепой,
К повороту, несмотря на то что
Тотчас же сшибается с толпой.
Он приперт к стене ацетиленом,
Втоптан в грязь, и несмотря на то,
Трын-трава и — море по колено:
Дует дальше с той же прямотой.
Вон он бьется, обваривши харю,
За косою рамой фонаря
И уходит, вынырнув на паре
Торопливых крыл нетопыря.

У матросов, несмотря на пору
И порывы ветра с пустыря,
На дворе казармы — шум и споры
Этой темной ночью ноября.
Их галдит за тысячу, и каждым,
Точно в бурю вешний буерак,
Разворочен, взрыт и взбудоражен
И буграми поднят этот мрак.
Пахнет волей, мокрою картошкой,
Пахнет почвой, норками кротов,
Пахнет штормом, несмотря на то что
Это шторм в открытом море ртов.

SECOND PART

1

Seized and freed from the waves, the breeze saunters
And gropes like a blind man who plods
Past the post office just round the corner
There colliding head on with the throng.
Pinned back against walls by acetylene
Stamped and trampled hard down in the mud,
What the hell, it's in sea knee-deep treading
Wafting onwards as bluntly it thrusts.
Muzzles scourging and scalding then surging
Off behind the skewed structure of lamps.
Off it flies, having just broken surface
Headlong borne upon swift wings of bats.

For the sailors in spite of the weather
And those rushes of wind from the wastes
Captured by this wild night in November
Yard and barracks shout loud in debate.
For each voice of that thousand-strong rumpus
By some springtime storm's gullying brook
Is dug up, churned over and furrowed
To hoist higher that pitch dark on hooks.
What a scent of moist soil and fresh molehills
What a scent of free wills and wet spuds
What a scent of fierce gales sweeping over
Mouth-filled seas falling prey to their gusts.

Тары-бары, шутки балагура,
Слухи, толки, шарканье подошв
Так и ходят вкруг одной фигуры,
Как распространившийся падёж.

Ходит слух, что он у депутатов,
Ходит слух, что едет в комитет,
Ходит слух, — и вот как раз тогда-то
Нарастает что-то в темноте,
И, глуша раскатами догадки
И сметая со всего двора
Караулки, будки и рогатки,
Катится и катится ура.

С первого же сказанного слова
Радость покидает берега.
Он дает улечься ей, и снова
Удесятеряет ураган.
Долго с бурей борется оратор.
Обожанье рвется на простор.
Не словами — полной их утратой
Хочет жить и дышит их восторг.
Это объясненье исполинов,
Он и двор обходятся без слов.
Если с ними флаг, то он — малинов.
Если мрак за них, то он — лилов.
Всё же раз доносится: эскадра.
Это с тем, чтоб браться, да с умом.
И потом другое слово: завтра.
Это, верно, о себе самом.

Tittle-tattle and jests by smart quipsters,
Hearsay, gossip and chat circulate
Amid soles scraping round a lone figure
To spread fast as a virulent plague.

Talk is rife that he's in the commission
Talk is rife that he's off to the branch
Talk is rife – but at that very instant
Something's mounting up amid the dark.
Drowning out with thunder-claps these riddles
Sweeping from its path across the yard
Roadblocks, guardposts, checkpoints and a pillbox
Rolls and rolls that wave of bold hurrahs.

Once the opening phrases have been uttered
Joyful moods abandon fast the shore.
Settling down until a further upsurge
Tenfold swells the hurricane once more.
Locked in strife the speaker tests the tempest.
Rapt adoration breaks into the space.
Such ecstasy begs him no long addresses
It leads him straight ahead without their aid.
For such the confrontation of two giants.
He and the yard get by with no words said.
When the gloom's behind him he seems lilac.
Carrying flags they turn him raspberry-red.
Sounds still reach their ears: they're from the squadron.
Signs to get things started, that makes sense.
After that, another word, tomorrow,
To be said in private, to himself.

2

Дорожных сборов кавардак.
«Твоя» твердящая упрямо,
С каракулями на бортах,
Сырая сетка телеграммы.

«Мне тридцать восемь лет. Я сед.
Не обернешься, глядь — кондрашка».
И с этим об пол хлоп портплед,
Продернув ремешки сквозь пряжки.
И на карачках под диван,
Потом от чемодана к шкапу... —
Любовь, горячка, караван
Вещей, переселенных на пол.

Как вдруг звонок, и кабинет
В перекосившемся: о боже!
И рядом: «Папы дома нет».
И грохотанье ног в прихожей.

Но двери настежь, и в дверях:
«Я здесь. Я враг кровопролитья».
— «Тогда какой же вы моряк,
Какой же вы тогда политик?

Вы революцьонер? В борьбу
Не вяжутся в перчатках дамских».
— «Я собираюсь в Петербург.
Не убеждайте. Я не сдамся».

Shambolic scenes of packing bags
'Yours ever' obstinately insisted
The wet vest of the telegram
With borders trimmed in scrawls and scribbling.

'I'm thirty-eight years old. Gone grey.
Don't turn away, just look, a fumbler.'
His holdall slapped the floor in rage
As strap he threaded through the buckle.
Beneath the bed upon all fours
And afterwards from trunk to cupboard –
The train of objects took the floor
With love amid that feverish scurry.

Just then a ring, and then there winced
The study's muddle: 'O good heavens!'
And straight away: 'But dad's not in!'
Then shuffling feet around the entrance.

But on the threshold, door's ajar:
'I'm here, an enemy of bloodshed'.
'A sailor that way won't get far
A politician that way hopeless.

Are you a rebel? Seems absurd,
For ladies' gloves don't square with fighting.'
'Well, no I'm off to Petersburg.
So don't dissuade me. I've decided.'

3

Подросток реалист,
Разняв драпри, исчез
С запиской в глубине
Отцова кабинета.
Пройдя в столовую
И уши навострив,
Матрос подумал:
«Хорошо у Шмидта».

Было это в ноябре,
Часу в четвертом.
Смеркалось.
Скромность комнат
Спорила с комфортом.
Минуты три извне
Не слышалось ни звука
В уютной, как каюта,
Конуре.

Лишь по кутерьме
Пылинок в пятерне портьеры,
Несмело шмыгавших
По книгам, по кошме
И окнам запотелым,
Видно было:
Дело —
К зиме.
Минуты три извне
Не слышалось ни звука
В глухой тиши, как вдруг
За плотными драпри
Проклятья раздались
Так явственно,
Как будто тут внутри:

A modern student youth,
Parts the curtains' pleats
With note in hand to plunge
Lost deep in father's study.
Into the diner moving
As ears he starts to prick,
The sailor briefly muses
'Seems all right at Schmidt's'

All this was round November time,
Say, four o' clockish.
Light's fading,
Comfort's bothered
By those rooms so rude and modest.
Three minutes from the street
Unheard the slightest patter
A kennel like a cabin,
Snug and neat.

Only from fine dusty specks
A-flurry through the doorman's fingers
And scampering so shyly
Across the books and felt
To dart past sweating windows
Would you tell
It's winter's
Spell.
Three minutes from the street
Unheard the slightest patter
In depths of silence when
Beyond the curtain's wall
Rose fulminating roars
So clearly heard
As if right here indoors.

— Чухнин! Чухнин?!
Погромщик бесноватый!
Виновник всей брехни!
Разоружать суда?
Нет, клеветник,
Палач,
Инсинуатор,
Я научу тебя, отродье ката, отличать
От правых виноватых!

Я Черноморский флот, холоп и раб,
Забью тебе, как кляп, как клепку, в глотку.
И мигом ока двери комнаты вразлет.
Буфет, стаканы, скатерть...
— Катер?
— Лодка!
В ответ на брошенный вопрос — матрос,
И оба — вон, очаковец за Шмидтом,
Невпопад, не в ногу, из дневного понемногу в ночь,
Наугад куда-то, вперехват закату,
По размытым рытвинам садовых гряд.
В наспех стянутых доспехах
Жарких полотняных лат,
В плотном, потном, зимнем платье
С головы до пят,
В облака, закат и эхо
По размытым, сбитым плитам
Променад.

Потом бегом. Сквозь поросли укропа,
Опрометью с оползня в песок,
И со всех ног, тропой наискосок
Кругом обрыва. Топот, топот, топот,
Топот, топот, — поворот — другой —
И вдруг как вкопанные, стоп:
И вот он, вот он весь у ног,
Захлебывающийся Севастополь,

'Chukhnin! Chukhnin?!
Vile thug, damned raving sadist!
Foul demon of deceit!
You'd like the ships disarming?
No, slanderous fiend
And rascal,
Calumniator,
Now I'll teach you, hangman, butcher. How we treat
The really guilty parties!

I, serf and slave, will stick the Black Sea fleet
Right down your gullet like a gag or rivet.'
The doors to his room flew open in a twinkling,
Glassware, tablecloth and kitchen ...
'Launches?'
'Boat's there!'
The sailor from the question thus casts off.
Both, with Schmidt there ran the man from *Ochakov*,
Out of step and place with daytime and just nightwards,
At random somewhere out astride the sundown,
Down washed-out ruts of garden plots,
Fastening fast their armour,
Hot linen breast-plates,
In winter garb so close and clammy
From head to toe,
To clouds that echo twilight's darkness
Down washed-out heel-worn flagstones
For a stroll.

And then they run. Through fennel shoots' green matting
From landslides sandwards charging both headlong
Along a slantwise pathway at full tilt
To skirt that steep defile. Then tramping, tramping,
Tramping, tramping round another turn.
Halt there, to the spot they're pinned,
And there she lies, at their feet flops all
Of panting, gasping, choking Sevastopol,

Весь вобранный, как воздух, грудью двух
Бездонных бухт,
И полукруг
Затопленного солнца за «Синопом».
С минуту оба переводят дух
И кубарем с последней кручи — бух
В сырую груду рухнувшего бута.

4

В зимней призрачной красе
Дремлет рейд в рассветной мгле,
Сонно кутаясь в туман
Путаницей мачт
И купаясь, как в росе,
Оторопью рей
В серебре и перламутре
Полумертвых фонарей.
Еле-еле лебезит
Утренняя зыбь.
Каждый еле слышный шелест,
Чем он мельче и дряблей,
Отдается дрожью в теле
Кораблей.

Он спит, притворно занедужась,
Могильным сном, вогнав почти
Трехверстную округу в ужас.
Он спит, наружно вызвав штиль.
Он скрылся, как от колотушек,
В молочно-белой мгле. Он спит
За пеленою малодушья.
Но чем он с панталыку сбит?
С утра на суше — муравейник.
В тумане тащатся войска.
Всего заметней их роенье
Толпе у Павлова мыска.

Like air, inhaled and gulped by two deep chests
Of floorless gulfs
And scuttled sun
Whose semi-circle's aft the *Sinop*.
For just a moment both remain quite puffed:
Then, somersaulting down the final hump
They plump down damp on dumps of crumbling rubble.

4

Winter's here with spectral grace,
Roads slumber in the daybreak's haze,
Drowsing swathed deep in the mist
Of masts' meshed tangled twists
And the dew-drenched yard-arms bathe
Dumbstruck and bereft of wits
In the nacre and the silver
Of the lanterns' half-dead glints.
The ripples of the morning tide
Barely, barely creep and cringe.
Every scarcely stirring whisper,
All their splintered fragile chips
Echo in those hulls' mute quivers
From the ships.

He sleeps, with some purported sickness,
Sepulchral sleep that struck alarm
Into that almost three-verst vista.
He sleeps, producing outward calm.
He's hidden, fleeing watchmen's clappers,
In milk-white haziness. He sleeps
Beneath a cowardly shroud caught napping
But what has put him in this dream?
An anthill on the shore since morning.
The forces trudge on through the fog.
They most conspicuously crawl swarming
Among the throng on Pavlov's knoll.

Пехотный полк из Павлограда
С тринадцатою полевой
Артиллерийскою бригадой
И — проба потной мостовой.

Колеса, кони, пулеметы,
Зарядных ящиков разбег,
И — грохот, грохот до ломоты
Во весь Нахимовский проспект.
На Историческом бульваре,
Куда на этих днях свезен
Военный лом былых аварий, —
Донцы и Крымский дивизион.

И любопытство, любопытство:
Трехверстный берег под тупой,
Пришедшей пить или топиться,
Тридцатитысячной толпой.

Она покрыла крыши барок
Кишащей кашей черепах,
И ковш Приморского бульвара,
И спуска каменный черпак.
Он ею доверху унизан,
Как копотью несметных птиц,
Копящих силы по карнизам,
Чтоб вихрем гари в ночь нестись.

Когда сбежали испаренья
И солнце, колыхнувши флот,
Всплыло на водяной арене,
Как обалдевший кашалот,
В очистившейся панораме
Обрисовался в двух шагах
От шара — крейсер под парами,
Как кочегар у очага.

From Pavlograd infantry troopers
With them the thirtieth brigade
Whose files of field artillery units
Test out on sweaty roads their weight.

All wheels and horses and machine-guns
To ammo-waggons' limbering step
All roar and rumble, puncturing eardrums
The length of Nakhimov Prospekt.
On Grand Istoricheskii Boulevard
To start the act they've now brought on
Those past disasters' martial crowbars,
Divisions from Crimea and Don.

Agape they stand, agape and gawping:
That baffled thirty-thousand crowd
Beneath them lies that three-verst shoreline
Beneath those come to drink or drown.

It overran the barges' bulwarks,
A teeming tortoise-seeming gruel,
And ladle-like Primorskii Boulevard
And the quayside ramp's stone scoop.
It has been lowered brimming over
As if with soot of countless birds
Rallying forces round high stonework
For night's winged charge in cindery whirls.

And when the fumes and fog had fallen
The sun to which the vessels sway
Broke surface on that stage of water,
A truly stunned and stricken whale.
Into that mopped horizon fusing
Two paces from that orb profiled
Beneath the vapours lay the cruiser
Just like a poker by the fire.

5

Вдруг, как снег на голову, гул
Толпы, как залп, стегнул
Трехверстовой гранит
И откатился с плит.
Ура — ударом в борт, в штурвал,
В бушприт!
Ура навеки, наповал,
Навзрыд!
Над крейсером взвился сигнал:
КОМАНДУЮ ФЛОТОМ. ШМИДТ.

Он вырвался как вздох
Со дна души рядна,
И не его вина,
Что не предостерег
Своих, и их застиг врасплох,
И рвется, в поисках эпох,
В иные времена.

Он вскинут, как магнит
На нитке, и на миг
Щетинит целый лес вестей
В осиннике снастей.

Над крейсером взвился сигнал:
КОМАНДУЮ ФЛОТОМ. ШМИДТ.

И мачты рейда, как одна:
Он ими вынесен и смыт
И перехвачен второпях
На двух — на трех — на четырех
Военных кораблях.

Like snow on heads came sudden falls
The three-verst granite shore
By volleying throngs is whipped
From pavements then to slip.
Hurrah, a shot which struck well fore
The bridge!
Hurrah for ever, retorted all
And wept.
Above the cruiser signals soared:
COMMANDING ALL THE NAVY, SCHMIDT.

Burst canvas from the hold.
It cannot be his fault,
That he has not yet warned
(Sighs sail-like from his soul)
His men caught wholly on the hop
Seeking epochs lost
Back into days of yore.

Just like a magnet on a string
And for one instant twitched
A wholesale growth of news then bristles
In aspens of equipment.

Above the cruiser signals soared:
COMMANDING ALL THE NAVY, SCHMIDT.

And, just as one, masts in the road
Then brought them forth and washed them clean.
In haste snatched up and swapped and thrown
Between the ships, first two, then three,
Four vessels they bestrode.

Но иссякает ток подков,
И облетает лес флажков,
И по веревке, как зверек,
Спускается кумач:
А зверь, ползущий на флагшток,
Ужасен, как немой толмач,
И флаг Андреевский — томящ,
Как рок.

6

Когда с остальными увидел и Шмидт,
Что только медлительность мига хранит
Бушприт и канаты
От града и надо
Немедля насытить его аппетит,
Чтоб только на миг оттянуть канонаду,
В нем точно проснулся дремавший Орфей.
И что ж он задумал, другого первей?
Объехать эскадру,
Усовестить ядра,
Растрогать стальные созданья верфей.

И на миноносце ушел он туда,
Где, небо и гавань ловя в невода,
В снастях, бездыханной
Семьей богдыханов,
Династией далей дымились суда.
Их строй был поистине неисчислим.
Грядой пристаней не граничился клин,
Но, весь громоздясь Пелионом на Оссу,
Под лад броненосцам
Качался и несся
Обрывистый город в шпалерах маслин.

But as the horseshoes staunched ther flow,
In flight they shun that pennants' grove
And, snake-like, down the rope, there droop
Red, calico-made kites.
And, flag-pole borne, the creature looms
As fearful as a tongueless guide,
While Andrew's ensign flags and tires,
Foredoomed.

6

To Schmidt and the others it all seemed quite plain,
That only the moment's inertia has saved
The foremast and cable
From downpours of hailstones.
His appetite he had to sate straight away,
Just for one second to put off the volleys
As if he is Orpheus fast roused from his sleep.
Why not be the first?, so to him it now seems.
Review all the squadron
Thus urge the men onwards
And stir the grey shipyards' creations of steel.

On board a torpedo-boat there he made speed,
To where skyline and harbour get caught up in seines
And tackle of panting,
Proud mandarin families,
In distances' dynasties warships raised steam.
Incalculably lay strict formations of vessels
Unedged by long ridges of wharves in a wedge,
But Pelion topped Ossa, her summit outstripping,
To the battleships' singing
Towered rocking and skimming
The steep-trellised city on olive-tree frets.

Он тихо шел от пушки к пушке,
А даль неслась.
Он шел под взглядами опухших,
Голодных глаз.

И вот, стругая воду, будто
Стальной терпуг,
Он видел не толпу над бухтой,
А Петербург.

Но что могло напомнить юность?
Неужто сброд,
Грязнивший слух, как сток гальюнный
Для нечистот?

С чужих бортов друзья по школе,
Тех лет друзья,
Ругались и встречали в колья,
Петлей грозя.

Назад! Зачем соваться под нос,
Под дождь помой?
Утратят ли боеспособность
«Синоп» с «Чесмой»?

From gun to gun he quietly strolled on.
The distance drifts.
He strolled beneath their weary swollen
Weak famished lids.

No crowd saw he above that inlet
Instead it seemed
He planed the waves past Peter's city
Filed smooth with steel.

How's he reminded by that riff-raff
Of youthful days.
They soiled his hearing like a shit-pipe
Disgorging waste.

From alien decks friends from past meetings
Old chums from school,
Were swearing and with stakes ran greeting
Him with a noose.

Back! Why're you meddling, why're you snooping
Well flushed with bilge?
So are *Chesma* and *Sinop* losing
Their fighting trim?

8

Снова, на миг повернувшись круто,
Город от криков задрожал:
На миноносец брали с «Прута»
Освобожденных каторжан.
Снова, приветствуем экипажем,
На броненосцы всходил и глох
И офицеров брал под стражу
И уводил с собой в залог.

В смене отчаянья и отваги
Вновь, озираясь, мертвел, как холст:
Всюду суда тасовали флаги.
Стяг государства за красным полз.
По возвращеньи же на «Очаков»,
Искрой надежды еще согрет,
За волоса схватясь, заплакал,
Как на ладони увидев рейд.

«Эх, — простонал, — без ножа доконали!»
Натиском зарев рдела вода.
Дружно смеркалось. Рейд удлиняли
Тучи, косматясь, как в холода.
С суши, в порыве низкопоклонства,
Шибче, чем надо, как никогда,
Падали крыши складов и консульств,
Камни и тени, скалы и солнце
В воду и вечность, как невода.
Всё закружилось так, что в финале
Обморок сшиб его без труда.

Again, one moment turning quickly,
The city shuddered at the shrieks:
Torpedo-boats from *Prut* are bringing
Imprisoned sailors now released.
Now by his crew he's once more welcomed
Upon the dreadnought tongue-tied embarked,
As hostages those officers held there
Were taken by him under guard.

In place of both despair and valour
Once more looked round, froze stiff as death:
Everywhere ships shuffled banners
Imperial flags crept over red.
Returning to the *Ochakov*
Flickering still with sparks of hope
He tore his hair out, started weeping
As at close range he watched the roads.

'Ugh!' he groaned out, 'you've dumped me, you tricksters!'
Water shone red in onslaughts of glows.
Twilight closed in. Clouds shaggily shivered
Coldstruck they bristled and stretched out the roads.
Landwards in fits of crass sycophancy
Needlessly speeding, then fast fell his hopes,
Depots and consulate rooftops collapsed.
Into a sweepnet too hurriedly sagging
Drowned by eternity's shadows and stones.
When by the closing round all started spinning
Faintness knocked him promptly to the ropes.

9

Был выспренен, как сердце,
И тих закат, как вдруг
Метнула пушка с «Терца»
Икру.

Мгновенный взрыв котельной,
Далекий крик с байдар,
И — под воду. Смертельный
Удар!

От катера к шаландам
Пловцы, тела, балласт.
И радость: часть команды
Спаслась.

И началось. Пространства,
Клубясь, метнулись в бой,
Чтоб пасть и опростаться
Пальбой.

His heart sank like the sunset
So silent and so vain
When from the *Terets* gunner
Spawn's laid.

An instant blasts the boiler,
From kayaks distant cries,
To plumb the waves. One mortal
Last strike.

Towards the scows from launches
Edge ballast, swimmers, dead.
Saved from the crew, what joy now,
Some men.

And thus it started. Spaces,
In spirals joined the fray,
Once smitten by guns blazing,
Fell drained.

10

Внутри настала ночь. Снаружи
Зарделся движущийся хвост
Над войском всех родов оружья
И свойств.

Он лез, грабастая овраги,
И треском разгонял толпу,
И пламенел, и гладил флаги
По лбу.

Как сумерки, сгустились снасти.
В ревущей, хлещущей дряпне
Пошла валить, как снег в ненастье,
Шрапнель.

Она рвалась, в лету, на жнивьях,
В расцвете лет людских, в воде,
Рождая смерть, и визг, и вывих
Везде

Inside night fell. Outside advancing
There reddened and hung down a tail
Of men and weapons of all classes
And grades.

It crept up, snatching, clinching chasms
And with a crackle split that crowd,
And, flaming, flattened out the flagpoles
To ground.

Like twilight, vessels' rigging densened.
In groaning, gushing shreds dropped low
Thick shrapnel falls just as foul weather
Drops snow.

On stubble fields it tore down racing
Into the water and youth's flower,
To death gave birth, mid screams and mayhem
All round.

ЧАСТЬ ТРЕТЬЯ

1

«Всё отшумело. Вставши поодаль,
Чувствую всею силой чутья:
Жребий завиден. Я жил и отдал
Душу свою за други своя.

Высшего нет. Я сердцем — у цели
И по пути в пустяках не увяз.
Крут был подъем, и сегодня, в сочельник,
Ошеломляюсь, остановясь.

Но объясни. Полюбив даже вора,
Как не рвануться к нему в каземат
В дни, когда всюду только и спору,
Нынче его или завтра казнят?

Ты ж предпочла омрачить мне остаток
Дней. Прости мне эти слова.
Спор подогнал бы таянье святок.
Лучше задержим бег рождества.

Где он, тот день, когда, вскрыв телеграмму,
Всё позабыв за твоим «навсегда»,
Жил я мечтой, как помчусь и нагряну?
Как же, ты скажешь, попал я сюда?

В вечер ее полученья был митинг.
Я предрекал неуспех мятежа,
Но уж ничто не могло вразумить их.
Ехать в ту ночь означало бежать.

THIRD PART

1

'All's faded fast. Then aloof I arose,
Sensing myself down to the very quick:
Enviable fortune. Devoting my soul,
Laying my life down for my friends to live.

Not ever swamped on the way by mere trivia,
Heart on the target, there's no higher aim.
Steep was the climb and today before Christmas
Waiting to rest, I feel suddenly dazed.

But just explain, befriending those robbers,
How could I not break through to their cells,
In those days when everywhere there were but quarrels
Whether tomorrow or now hears their knells.

You, though, preferred to make them all gloomy,
Forgive me my words, to cloud life's remains.
Our own row would then catch the snap thaw at
    Yuletide.
Best to defer such a Christmas escape.

So where's that day when opening your cable
All fell forgotten behind your 'farewell'?
How should I act or proceed, living daydreams?
How, you will ask me, am I here in hell.

Meetings were held the same day I received it.
I had foreseen no success for revolt,
Nothing however could make them see reason.
Travelling that night would mean simply to bolt.

О, как рвался я к тебе! Было пыткой
Браться и знать, что народ не готов,
Жертвовать встречей и видеть в избытке
Доводы в пользу других городов.

Вера в разъезд по фабричным районам,
В новую стачку и новый подъем,
Может, сплеталась во мне с затаенным
Чувством, что ездить будем вдвоем.

Но повалила волна депутаций,
Дума, эсдеки, звонок за звонком.
Выехать было нельзя и пытаться.
Вот и кончаю бунтовщиком,

Кажется, всё. Я гораздо спокойней,
Чем ожидают. Что бишь еще?
Да, а насчет севастопольской бойни,
В старых газетах — полный отчет».

Oh, how I longed just for you! It was torture
Starting off when the crowds weren't prepared
Standing you up as I saw all the courses
Swung me in favour of cities elsewhere.

Faith in a tour of industrial districts
In a fresh strike and an upswing renewed
Deep within me may have fused for an instant
With a deep urge to go off, we two.

But deputations like waves kept on breaking.
Duma types and social democrats rang.
No good attempting to go off campaigning
So I end leading a mutinous gang.

Seems that's the lot. I am now so much calmer,
Than they expected. So what on earth else?
Yes, for full news of Sevastopol's carnage
Read the back numbers — it's all in the press.'

2

Послепогромной областью почтовый поезд в Ро́мны
Сквозь вопли вьюги доблестно прокладывает путь.
Снаружи — вихря гарканье, огарков проблеск темный,
Мигают гайки жаркие, на рельсах пляшет ртуть.
Огни и искры чиркают, и дым над изголовьем
Бежит за пассажиркою по лестницам витым.
В одиннадцать, не вынеся немолчного злословья,
Она встает, и — к выходу на вызов клеветы.

И молит, в дверь просунувшись: «Прошу вас,
                                        не шумите...
Нельзя же до полуночи!» И разом в лязг и дым
Уносит оба голоса и выдумку о Шмидте,
И вьет и тащит по́ лесу, по лестницам витым.
Наверно, повод есть у ней, отворотясь к простенку,
Рыдать, сложа ответственность в сырой комок
                                        платка.
Вы догадались, кто она. — Его корреспондентка.
В купе кругом рассованы конверты моряка.

А в ту же ночь в Очакове в пурге и мыльной пене
Полощет створки раковин песчаная коса.
Постройки есть на острове, острог и укрепленье.
Он весь из камня острого, и — чайки на часах.
И неизвестно едущей, что эта крепость-тезка
(Очаков — крестный дедушка повстанца корабля)
Таит по злой иронии звезду надежд матросских,
От взора постороннего прибоем отделя.

The mail train bound for Romny, over pogrom-ravaged regions,
Lays boldly out its track across the blizzards' howling wails.
Outside, to whirlwinds' barking, candle-stubs are darkly gleaming
The red-hot nuts are twinkling, mercury dances on the rails.
Far lights and sparks strike matches, inside, above her
    headboard dropping
Down spiral stairs, our passenger's pursued by swirling smoke.
Eleven's struck, she simply can't abide that endless gossip
So gets up and goes out, to stop that slander she's provoked.

She begs, her head poked round the door: 'Please, please,
    don't be so noisy. . .
'You can't say that it's not yet midnight!' By the smoke and din
Those yarns of Schmidt are dragged away along with both
    those voices
Down spiral stairways through the forest swept into a spin.
Of course she has good cause to lean against the window sobbing
Discharging guilty thoughts upon her hankie's dampening lump.
You've guessed right who she is: the girl with whom he's
    corresponding
With sailor's envelopes her compartment has been overrun.

But that same night on Ochakov is driving snow and lather
The folding wings of shells are rinsed out by a sandy spit.
On the island stand some structures, dungeons well ramparted
All built of sharp-hewn stone, upon the clockface seagulls sit.
The passenger is unaware that fortress is the namesake
(Ochakov was the god-grandfather of the rebel's ship).
Concealing by true irony the guiding star of sailors
Which from the gaze of passers-by the surf-trimmed breakers hid.

Но что пред забастовкою почтово-телеграфной
Все тренья и неловкости во встрече двух сердец!
Теперь хоть бейся о́б стену в борьбе с судьбой
                                              неравной,
Дознаться, где он, собственно, нет ни малейших
                                              средств.

До Ромен не доехать ей. Не скрыться от мороки.
Беглянка видит нехотя: забвенья нет в езде,
И пешую иль бешено катящую, с дороги
Ее вернут депешею к ее дурной звезде.

Тогда начнутся поиски, и происки, и слезы,
И двери тюрем вскроются, и, вдоволь очернив,
Сойдутся посноровистей объятья пьяной прозы,
И смерть скользнет по повести, как оттиск пятерни.
И будет день посредственный, и разговор в передней
И обморок, и шествие по лестнице витой,
И тонущий в периодах, как камень, миг последний,
И жажда что-то выудить из прорвы прожитой.

For though before the general telegraph and postal stoppage
Such stresses and embarrassments fed meetings of two hearts!
In destiny's unequal fight, against brick walls she's
    knocking.
Of finding out just where he is, she's not the slightest
    chance.
She'll not arrive at Romny. She can't elude that drawn-out hassle
As, on the run, she has to see, oblivion's not in flight,
And, whether off on foot or, wildly steaming, from her travels
She'll like a dispatch be returned to face her sorry plight.

And then the searches, scheming and the tears find their beginning
With prison doors flying open and his name made truly black,
His drunken prose's firm embrace will close round you more nimbly,
And death will slide across the tale, imprinting like a hand,
An average day will come with conversations in the hallway,
Processions down the spiral stairs and then a sudden faint
Until the final instant, into epochs stone-like falling
With thirst to fish just something out from shoals of bygone days.

3

Как памятен ей этот переход!
Приезд в Одессу ночью новогодней.
С какою неохотой пароход
Стал поднимать в ту непогоду сходни!
И утренней картины не забыть.
В ушах шумело море горькой хиной.
Снег перестал, но продолжали плыть
Обрывки туч, как кисти балдахина.

Потом вдали из кучки пирамид
Привстал маяк поганкою мухортой.
«Мадам, вот остров, где томится Шмидт»,
И публика шагнула вправо к борту.
Когда пороховые погреба
Зашли за строй бараков карантинных,
Какой-то образ трупного гриба
Остался гнить от виденной картины.

Понурый, хмурый, черный островок
Несло водой, как шляпку мухомора.
Кружась в водовороте, как плевок,
Он затонул от полного измора.
Тем часом пирамиды из химер
Слагались в город, становились тверже
И вдруг, застлав слезами глазомер,
Образовали крепостные горжи.

3

How memorable for her that crossing is!
On New Year's Eve arriving in Odessa.
With what reluctance did the boat begin
To raise its gangplank in such squally weather.
That morning's scene she never could forget.
Her ears throbbed hard with seas of bitter quinine.
The snow had stopped but stormclouds torn to shreds
Like tassels of a canopy still drifted.

Then out from pyramids stacked up in piles
There loomed the bay-hued toadstool of a lighthouse.
'There, madam, is the island where Schmidt lies',
The passengers surge over for a sighting.
Just when those sombre powder magazines
Behind the quarantine sheds descended
A sort of stink-horn's form could be seen
Which from that view began to rot and fester.

The island, so dejected, black and dull
Lay waterlogged — like death-cap's lethal fungus.
It swirled like spit in eddies, then was sunk
Once fully stunned by pangs of utter hunger.
From pyramids the town's profile appears
As firm outlines emerge from what seemed monsters,
But then her eyes are overcast with tears,
And forms of fortress gorges show their contours.

4

Однако, как свежо Очаков дан у Данта!
Амбары, каланча, тачанки, облака…
Всё это так, но он дорогой к коменданту,
В отличье от нее, имел проводника.

Как ткнуться? Что сказать? Перебрала оттенки.
«Я — конфидентка Шмидта? Я — его дневник?
Я — крик его души из номеров Ткаченки,
Вот для него цветы и связка старых книг?

Удобно ли тогда с корзиной гиацинтов,
Не значась в их глазах ни в браке, ни в родстве?» —
Так думала она, и ветер рвал косынку
С земли, и даль неслась за крепостной бруствер.

Но это всё затмил прием у генерала.
Индюшачий кадык спирал сухой коклюш.
Желтел натертый пол, по окнам темь ныряла,
И снег махоркой жег больные глотки луж.

4

And yet how fresh a sketch Ochakov finds in Dante!
Low granaries, a watch tower, country carts and clouds . . .
All this is so, although his road's the commandancy's
For, as opposed to her, he travelled in a crowd.

How reach him? What to say? She sifted through
    nuances.
'I hold his diary? I'm the confidante of Schmidt?'
Or 'I'm his spirit's cry from Tkachenko's apartments,
See here, I've flowers for him and sheaves of dog-eared
    scripts?

Perhaps more apt to bring a basketful of hyacinths,
To relatives or marriage they'd then give little thought?'
As thus she mused, the wind whisked up her
    kerchief's triangle
And skylines darted past the parapet of the fort.

Eclipsed was all this though when welcomed by the
    general,
Whose turkeyish Adam's apple was with dry
    whooping choked.
Down windows dived the darkness to tint the parquet
    yellow
As dusk smoked shag to scorch the puddles' morbid
    throats.

5

Уездная глушь захолустья.
Распев петухов по утрам,
И холостящий устье
Весенний флюс Днепра.
Таким дрянным городишкой
Очаков во плоти
Встает, как смерть, притихши
У шмидтовцев на пути.

Похоже, с лент матросских
Сошедши без следа,
Он стал землей в отместку
И местом для суда.
Две крепости, два погоста
Да горсточка халуп,
Свиней и галок вдосталь
И офицерский клуб.

Без преувеличенья
Ты слышишь в эту тишь,
Как хлопаются тени
С пригретых солнцем крыш.
И звякнет ли шпорами ротмистр,
Прослякотит ли солдат,
В следах их — соли подмесь.
Вся отмель — точно в сельдях.

О, суши воздух ковкий,
Земли горячий фарш!
«Караул, в винтовки!
Партия, шагом марш!»
И, вбок косясь на приезжих,
Особым скоком сорок
Сторонится побережье
На их пути в острог.

Deep in some far-flung district
Each morning cockcrows swell.
Castrating spates
The Dnieper's outflow geld.
As such a wretched rotten village
There Ochakov arose
In flesh, now, like death, whispered,
By Schmidt's folk on the road.

Off sailors' ribbons semblance
Of that name, seems wiped clean,
It's been usurped in vengeance
To grace the trial's scene.
Two churchyards and two bastions
A handful of rude huts
Swine and quite some jackdaws
And officers at the club.

It's not hard to imagine
That heard amid that hush
Are dangling shadows flapping
From roofs kept snug by sun.
The captain's spurs are clicking
Then men he soaks in sludge,
Their tracks a salty mish-mash.
The shoals — a herring flood.

O shoreward air so pliant,
Warn forcemeat of the land!
'Guards, take up now your rifles!
'Quick march, you hapless band!'
Obliquely seen approaching
Then with a magpie's hop
They're sidestepped by the coastline
As bound for jail they plod.

О, воздух после трюма,
И высадки триумф!
Но в этот час угрюмый
Ничто нейдет на ум.
И горько, как на расстанках,
Качают головой
Заборы, арестанты,
И кони, и конвой.

Прошли, — и в двери с бранью
Костяшками бьет тишина...
Военного собранья
Фисташковая стена.
Из зал выносят мебель.
В них скоро ворвется гул.
Два писаря. Фельдфебель.
Казачий подъесаул.

O triumph of the landfall,
From hold to air they climb!
But in that day's dark shadow
Not one thing comes to mind.
As bitter as leave-taking,
The captives and the horse
All heads trace sadly shaking
The convoy's fence-edged course.

And through the doors with blather
There silence knuckles raps. . .
As serried brasshats gather
In one pistacchio bank.
Din surges in rampaging,
As chairs go from the hall
Two clerks. A sergeant-major.
A cossack sub-esaul.

6

Над Очаковом пронес
Ветер тучу слез и хмари
И свалился на базаре
Наковальнею в навоз.

И, на всех остервенясь,
Дождик, первенец творенья,
Горсть за горстью, к горсти горсть,
Хлынул шумным увереньем
В снег и грязь, в снег и грязь,
На зиму остервенясь.

А немного погодя,
С треском расшатавши крючья,
Шлепнулся и всею тучей
Водяной бурдюк дождя.

Этот странный талисман,
С неба сорванный истомой,
Весь — туманного письма,
Рухнул вниз не по-пустому.
Каждым всклипом он прилип
К разрывным побегам лип
Накладным листом пистона.
Хлопнуть вплоть, пропороть,
Выстрел, цвет, тепло и плоть.

Но зима не верит в близость,
В даль и смерть верит снег.
И седое небо, низясь,
Сыплет пригоршнями известь.
Это зимний катехизис
Шепчут хлопья в полусне.

On Ochakov the wind shit flung
Tearful nimbus and black cloudbanks,
As there collapsed on birds' nests' grounds that
Anvil thrusting into dung.

First-born of creation's rage,
Wrathful with the world, the downpours
Handful after handful landed
Noisy sure assertion spouting,
Snow, mud, rain, snow, mud, raid,
Within the winter's foul outrage.

Just a little longer wait,
With a crack of brackets slipping,
Black clouds shrouded all the dripping
Watery wineskins welling rain.

This the strangest talisman,
Plucked from heaven, ripped by languor,
All written in a foggy hand
Crashed straight down the weighty anger.
Every sob it sought to bind
To the lime-trees' fissile flights,
Overlaid, percussion-capping,
Slaps the ground, to death it flails
Warmth and flesh, all shots' shades.

Snow believes in death and distance,
Closeness wins not winter's faith.
And greying skies, as they're sprinkling
Lime in handfuls, lower're dipping.
This is winter's catechism,
Dozing quietly, whisper flakes.

И, шипя, кружит крупа
По́ небу и мертвой глине,
Но мгновенный вздох теплыни
Одевает черепа.

Пусть тоща, как щепа,
Вязь цветочного шипа,
Новолунью улыбаясь,
Как на шапке шалопая,
Сохнет краска голубая
На сырых концах серпа.

И, долбя и колупая
Льдины старого пласта,
Спит и ломом бьет по сини,
Рты колоколов разиня,
Размечтавшийся в уныньи
Звон великого поста.

Наблюдая тяжбу льда,
В этом звяканьи спросонья
Подоконниками тонет
Зал военного суда.

Всё живое беззаконье,
Вся душевная бурда
Из зачатий и агоний
В снеге, слякоти и звоне
Перед ним, как на ладони,
Ныне так же, как тогда.

Чем же занято собранье?
Казнью звали в те года
Переправу к Березани.
Современность просит дани:
Высшей мере наказанья
Служат эти господа.

Through the sky sweeps circling sleet,
Through the clay of death it hisses,
But the skulls are for one instant
Clothed and clad by sighs of heat.

Like a skinny, splintered chip,
Florid thorns in flowing scripts
At the new moon gaze up smiling
As at the cap of some old skiver,
Let the sky-blue paint glint drying
On that sickle's damp thin tips.

Ice-floes of an ancient stratum,
Gouged and ground with prising pecks
Azure tints with crows lambasted,
Gawking bell-mouths flabbergasting,
Tossing, turning, those downhearted
Sleeping peals of lenten bells.

Ice, observed being sent to court,
With its white half-waking tinkling
To its window-sills is sinking
Grimly that court martial's hall.

All of lawlessness that's living,
All the spirit's washed-out dregs
Rinsed from death-throes and foul instincts
In the snow and slush and ringing,
Now before them close impinges
Bilge and filth it is as then.

What's the aim of this assembly?
Is this then a call for death?
Berezan's swift trip by ferry.
Modern times seek recompensing:
Harshest steps, the supreme sentence
Shall be served upon these gents.

Скамьи, шашки, выпушка охраны,
Обмороки, крики, схватки спазм.
Чтенье, чтенье, чтенье; несмотря на
Головокруженье, несмотря
На пары нашатыря и пряный,
Пьяный запах слез и валерьяны,
Чтение без пенья тропаря,
Рама, и жандармы-ветераны,
Шаровары и кушак царя,
И под люстрой зайчик восьмигранный.

Чтенье, несмотря на то, что рано
Или поздно, сами, будет день,
Сядут там же за грехи тирана
В грязных клочьях поседелых пасм.
Будет так же ветрен день весенний,
Будет страшно стать живой мишенью,
Будут высшие соображенья
И капели вешней дребедень.
Будут схватки астмы. Будет чтенье,
Чтенье, чтенье без конца и пауз.

Версты обвинительного акта,
Шапку в зубы, только не рыдать!
Недра шахт вдоль Нерчинского тракта.
Каторга, какая благодать!
Только что и думать о соблазне.
Шапку в зубы — да минуй озноб!
Мысль о казни — топи непролазней:
С лавки съедешь, с головой увязнешь,
Двинешься, чтоб вырваться, и — хлоп.
Тормошат, повертывают навзничь,
Отливают, волокут, как сноп.

Benches, sabres, sentries decked in braiding,
Shouting, scuffling, fainting fits and starts.
Reading, reading, no regard for dazed and
Dizzy heads, with no regard
For sal-ammoniac's wafting vapours
And tear-tinged valerian's drunk spiced fragrance.
Reading yet with no responding chants,
Window-framed by veteran gendarmes waiting,
Sashes, sharovary from that tsar
Chandeliers beam octohedral traces.

Reading, no regard that sooner, later
For themselves, the court, the day will come
For the tyrant's sins, to sit arraigned there
Draped in dirty, grey, dishevelled locks.
Come one springtime day that's just as windy,
Come that fear when, under fire, they're living victims,
Come the highest reasons for conviction
With the trash of spring's thawed drips turned floods.
Come too fits of asthma. Come the reading,
Reading, reading with no pause nor stop.

Versts and versts long stretched the whole indictment.
Cap between your teeth, so not to cry!
Deep down mines along the Nerchinsk highway,
Penal servitude, what paradise!
Only just to think about the promise.
Careful, don't catch chills – bite your cap!
Thoughts of torture – of some quagmire
      swampbound:
Sliding off the bench, your heads well bogged down,
Slipping forward to break free, then wham!
Over on your back, you're poked and prodded,
Sheaf-like, poured out, promptly sacked and dragged.

В перерывах — таска на гауптвахту
Плотной кучей, в полузабытьи.
Ружья, лужи, вязкий шаг без такта,
Пики, гики, крики: осади!
Утки — крякать, курицы — кудахтать,
Свист нагаек, взбрызги колеи.
Это небо, пахнущее как-то
Так, как будто день, как масло, спахтан!
Эти лица, и в толпе — свои!
Эти бабы, плачущие в плахтах!
Пики, гики, крики: осади!

8

Кому-то стало дурно.
Казалось, жуть минуты
Простерлась от Кинбурна
До хуторов и фольварков
За мысом Тарканхутом.
Послышалось сморканье
Жандармов и охранников,
И жилы вздулись жолвями
На лбах у караульных.
Забывши об уставе,
Конвойные отставили
Полуживые ружья
И терли кулаками
Трясущиеся скулы.

При виде этой вольности
Кто-то безотчетно
Полез уж за револьвером,
Но так и замер в позе
Предчувствия чего-то,
Похожего на бурю,
С рукой на кобуре.

Stopping on the way – guardroom hair-tugging,
Semi-conscious, in crushed heaps they're thrown.
Muddy, clumsy marching, rifles, puddles,
Lances, bawling, whooping, steady, whoa!
Ducks a-quacking and the chickens clucking,
Hissing lashes, spatters from the road.
While the sky above is smelling just as
If it were a day churned into butter!
See the faces here, they are our own!
See the dames, in skirts cut square, eyes running!
Lances, bawling, whooping, steady, whoa!

8

Then someone felt quite queasy.
The minute's horror seemed then
To stretch away from Kinburn
Beyond Tarkankhut's headland
To farms and homesteads reaching.
Blown noses are heard snorting
From gendarmes and policemen,
And veins swelled out on foreheads
Form tumours on the sentries.
Forgetting all their orders,
With rifles semi-dormant
As fists are clenching, squeezing,
The now redundant escorts
Rub twitching, quaking cheekbones.

But at such sloppy conduct
Shocked, someone unofficially
Reached down for his revolver,
Froze stock-still in that posture
As if he had some inkling
Of some storm's distant rumble,
With hand his holster clutching.

Волнение предгрозья
Окуталось удушьем,
Давно уже идущим
Откуда-то от Ольвии.

И вот он поднялся.

Слепой порыв безмолвия
Стянул гусиной кожей
Тазы и пояса,
И, протащившись с дрожью,
Как зябкая оса,
По записям и папкам,
За пазухи и шапки
Заполз под волоса.

И точно шла работа
По сборке эшафота,
Стал слышен частый стук
Полутораста штук
Расколебавших сумрак
Пустых сердечных сумок.

Все были предупреждены,
Но это превзошло расчеты.
«Тише!» — крикнул кто-то,
Не вынесши тишины.

«Напрасно в годы хаоса
Искать конца благого.
Одним карать и каяться,
Другим — кончать Голгофой.

Как вы, я — часть великого
Перемещенья сроков,
И я приму ваш приговор
Без гнева и упрека.

Thunder's threatening onrush
Lay choked, asphyxia-muffled,
Yet long since had been coming
From somewhere out off Olvia.

At this point he got up.

A blinding blast that's speechless
To gooseflesh tightly squeezed in
Strapped pelvises in strops
And, trembling, it came creeping
Like a shivering wasp,
Through portmanteaux and records,
Past bosoms and peaked headgear
To slip beneath their locks.

A sound of work progressing
On scaffolds being erected,
Came from the frequent pulse
Of those one-fifty thumps
Of heartless gangs of vacuous
Shade-shaken cardiac cavities.

All had been carefully pre-ordained,
What came upset all firm arrangements.
'Silence!' shouted someone,
Who couldn't stand the silence.

'To seek in times chaotic
Good luck's an unreal option.
While some may rue and punish,
The rest land in Golgotha.

Like you, I lie extended
Through timescales well reshuffled,
But I'll accept your sentence
Reproachless and unruffled.

Наверно, вы не дрогнете,
Сметая человека.
Что ж, мученики догмата,
Вы тоже — жертвы века.

Я тридцать лет вынашивал
Любовь к родному краю,
И снисхожденья вашего
Не жду и не теряю.

Как непомерна разница
Меж именем и вещью!
Зачем Россия красится
Так явно и зловеще!

Едва народ по-новому
Сознал конец опеки,
Его от прав дарованных
Поволокли в аптеки.

Всё было вновь отобрано.
Так вечно пункт за пунктом
Намереньями добрыми
Доводят нас до бунта.

В те дни, — а вы их видели,
И помните, в какие, —
Я был из ряда выделен
Волной самой стихии.

Не встать со всею родиной
Мне было б тяжелее,
И о дороге пройденной
Теперь не сожалею.

For sure you will be trembling
At wiping out a mortal.
More victims of our century,
You act as dogma's martyrs.

My country till I'm thirty
Was nurtured by affection
But any sort of mercy
From you I'm not expecting.

So gaugeless then the gulf is
Mid object and its namesake!
So rouged her face our Russia
With evil airs so naked!

Once more the people hardly
Had felt their wardship ending,
When they from rights once granted
Were wrenched back to the chemists.

All was well picked and chosen
And point by point for ever
Our good intentions' road will
Lead us on to rebellion.

Those days that you've seen often,
And carefully remember
Brought me out from the common
Crowd by the very elements.

For me it would be harder
Not rising with my homeland,
So at that road I've passed down
There seems no point in moaning.

Поставленный у пропасти
Слепою властью буквы,
Я не узнаю робости,
И не смутится дух мой.

Я знаю, что столб, у которого
Я стану, будет гранью
Двух разных эпох истории,
И радуюсь избранью».

Upon the brink installed by
The writing's blind dominion,
Not knowing any qualms I'll
Calmly rest my spirit.

I know my post's a pillar
Where on the very border
Of two historic instants
I'll fete my chosen fortune'.

Двум из осужденных, а всех их было четверо, —
Думалось еще — из четырех двоим.
Ветер гладил звезды горячо и жертвенно
Вечным чем-то, чем-то зиждущим своим.

Распростившись с ними, жизнь брела по дамбе,
Удаляясь к людям в спящий городок.
Неизвестность вздрагивала плавниками камбалы.
Тихо, миг за мигом рос ее приток.

Близился конец, и не спалось тюремщикам.
Быть в тот миг могло примерно два часа.
Зыбь переминалась, пожирая жемчуг.
Так, чем свет, в конюшнях дремлет хруст овса.

Остальных пьянила ширь весны и каторги.
Люки были настежь, и точно у миног,
Округлясь, дышали рты иллюминаторов.
Транспорт колыхался, как сонный осьминог.

Вдруг по тьме мурашками пробежал прожектор.
«Прут» зевнул, втянув тысячеперстье лап.
Свет повел ноздрями, пробираясь к жертвам.
Заскрипели петли. Упал железный трап.

Это канонерка пристала к люку угольному.
Свет всадил с шипеньем внутрь свою иглу.
Клетку ослепило. Отпрянули испуганно.
Путаясь костями в цепях, забились вглубь.

Two of those condemned, in all they formed a foursome,
Thought and hoped still: it would be from four but two.
Stars were stroked by winds which sacrificially, warmly,
Shaping something all their own, eternal, blew.

Parting from them, pensive life strolled off down ditches,
Wandering far away to folk asleep in town.
Flattened by uncertainty, the flounders shake like swimmers.
Calmly inch by inch, fate's flux swelled up to drown.

Soon approaching doom no sleep allowed the prisoners.
Left by now to live for two hours at the most.
Pearls were gulped by rippling waves whose feet kept shifting.
Daybreak's stables sheltered the slumbering crunch of oats.

Drunk the rest at labour camps' and spring's expanses.
Hatchways lie ajar and mouths of portholes breathe,
Puffing, rounded outwards, just like those of lampreys.
Convict trains like sleepy octopuses heave.

Through the dark a searchlight sends its sudden shivers.
Furling thousand-fingered boughs, the 'Prut' gives yawns.
Twitching nostrils, light steals through towards the victims.
Hinges start to squeak. An iron ladder falls.

To that coaly hatch by now has moored a gunboat.
Light and hisses stabbed inside its frosted spire.
Dazzling all their cages, the captives drew back dumbstruck.
Tangling bones in chains, deep in the bowels they hide.

Но затем, не в силах более крепиться,
Бросились к решетке, колясь о сноп лучей
И крича: «Не мучьте! Кончайте, кровопийцы!» —
Потянулись с дрожью в руки палачей.

Счет пошел на миги. Крик: «Прощай, товарищи!» —
Породил содом. Прожектор побежал,
Окунаясь в вопли, по люкам, лбам и наручням,
И пропал, потушенный рыданьем каторжан.

Март 1926 — март 1927

Now, not having any longer strength to hold back,
Charging to the bars, they're stung by blinding strands,
Cries: 'Don't torture us, you vampires, get it over'
Trembling, they edged forward to the butchers' hands.

Calculations went awry. A shout: 'Farewell, our comrades!'
Hell was then let loose. The searchlight flashed and fled.
Swathed in wails, past hatches, handcuffs and past foreheads,
Snuffed, it dipped and dimmed, damped as the convicts wept.

March 1926 – March 1927

NOTES

First Part

Chapter 1 (page 3)
Schmidt first saw Zinaida Ivanovna Riesberg, who was to become his confidente in the third part of the poem, at Kiev racecourse on July 22 1905 while en route from the Danube where he was serving, to visit his older sister in the Crimea.

BATU KHAN (c.1200 - 1255) The Mongol leader and grandson of Genghiz Khan whose forces sacked Kiev in 1240.

Chapter 2 (page 5)
The first letter that Schmidt wrote to Riesberg on July 24 refers to his chance encounter on the train between Kiev and Darnitsa following the racecourse meeting with Riesberg.

The first, magazine, edition carried the title 'The First Letter' and was longer.

Schmidt's letter of 26 July followed this chapter in the first edition called 'A Letter about Squabbles'.

Chapter 3 (page 7)
The first part was inserted into the 1927, book, edition while the second part beginning 'Come on, let's get matters straight..' bore the title, 'A letter from Sevastopol' in the first publication.

Chapter 4 (page 13)
The general political strike of October 1905 reached Sevastopol around the fifteenth. Schmidt's funeral oration and mass oath-taking was made on October 20 at a mass funeral of six demonstrators shot by Tsarist police on the eighteenth at a demonstration on Primorskii Boulevard demanding the release of political detainees. 20,000 attended this funeral and the text of Schmidt's Oath' is as follows:

'We swear to them that we will never yield to anyone a single inch of the human rights we have won!
We swear to them that we shall pledge all our work, all our souls and our life itself for the preservation of our freedom!
We swear to them that we will commit all our free public activity to the good of the propertyless, working folk!

We swear to them that among us there shall be neither Jew nor Armenian, neither Pole nor Tartar but that we shall be equal, free brothers of great and free Russia!
We swear to them that if we are not given universal suffrage we shall again proclaim an all-Russian strike'

This chapter was first entitled 'The Elements' and was cut.

Chapter 5 (page 15)

On October 17 the Tsar signed a manifesto promising certain formal constitutional rights to the people which was to be regarded as the first gain of the revolution. The two lines from 'hereby granting the populace...' are a quote from its text. The words 'Ye'll find it if ye seek it' echo the Sermon on the Mount (Matt. 7:7, Luke 11:9). The first version of this chapter was entitled 'The Marseillaise' and was cut.

The first publication included between chapters 4 and 5 a further letter to Riesberg dated October 19 called 'A manly letter' in which Schmidt declares his initial decision to depart to join the strike movement in Sevastopol.

Chapter 6 (page 17)

On November 9 a mass demonstration in Sevastopol called for the release of the Potyomkin crew held prisoner on the *Prut*. This chapter was originally entitled 'A November Meeting'.

ANTONOVKA. A type of apple tree which bears a winter crop with a bittersweet flavour.

Chapter 7 (page 21)

On November 11 Rear Admiral Pisarevsky ordered the break-up of a mass meeting of sailors by two infantry companies. With junior captain Stein he planned firing a shot to provoke the sailors but this was forestalled by Petrov, a rating from the cruiser *Varyag* who shot Pisarevsky dead and wounded Stein. The incident sparked off the sailors' and workers' uprising at Sevastopol. Originally entitled 'Uprising'.

Chapter 8 (page 25)

In May 1926 after completing the original text of the First Part, Pasternak discovered the memoirs of one of Schmidt's younger sisters, Anna Isbasch which included this letter. As he felt it shed important new light on Schmidt's personality he added this chapter to the book edition of the poem of 1927. Schmidt was held captive on the retired battleship 'Three Patriarchs' from October 20 till November 3 for his address to the funeral rally on the 20th.

BARKOV, Ivan Semyonovich (1732-1768) a writer of obscene verse.

There was here in the first edition another of Schmidt's letters to his sister which was subsequently dropped.

Chapter 9 (page 29)
The Brest infantry regiment at this stage supported the insurgent sailors and workers of Sevastopol. This chapter was originally called 'Flight by Residents' and stood at the beginning of the Second Part.

'VARSHAVYANKA'. The revolutionary march to a tune originating from the Polish Rising of 1863 and with words by Vaclav Svencicki re-worked by Gleb Krzhizhanovsky in Butyrki jail in 1897. By 1905 it had been sung by demonstrating workers throughout Russia.

Second Part

Chapter 1 (page 33)
On November 12 the joint commission of insurgent sailors and revolutionary soldiers was formed in Sevastopol. The original publication carried the title 'At the Naval Barracks'.

Chapter 2 (page 37)
Based on the memoirs of Schmidt's son, this chapter was first entitled 'A Difficult Night' and was cut prior to the 1927 book edition. It relates to November 13 1905.

Chapter 3 (page 39)
Also drawn from the memoirs of Schmidt's son, Evgenii, then a pupil at a 'modern' (i.e. non-classical) gymnasium, this chapter originally bore the title 'Unveering Decision'.

CHUKHNIN. Vice-Admiral G.P. Chukhnin, commander of the Imperial Black Sea Fleet, noted for his ferocious reprisals against the 'Potyomkin' crew and other revolutionaries.

SINOP. A 10,250-ton battleship completed in 1887. It carried a complement of 560 and could be forced to 17 knots.

Chapter 4 (page 43)
The events of the night of November 13-14 were first presented under the title 'Northern Roads'.

Chapter 5 (page47)
Schmidt assumed command of the insurrection on the 14th. Originally with the title 'Raising the Flags', this chapter was cut before final publication.

Chapters 6-8 (page 49)
First entitled 'Touring the Squadron', this chapter was cut.

PELION, OSSA. The mountains in Greece which legend tells were heaped on Olympus by the giants in an attempt to scale heaven and defeat Zeus

CHESMA. A reconstructed battleship displacing 10,250 tons carrying a crew of 530 and cruising at 15 knots.

PRUT. A training vessel converted into a floating prison which held convicted mutineers from the 'Potyomkin'.

OCHAKOV. A fast cruiser of 6,750 tons completed at Sevastopol in 1905 which carried 573 crew and could reach 23 knots. It was Schmidt's command post.

Chapter 9-10 (page 55)
The rising was militarily finally crushed by 5.00am on November 16 1905 following which some 400 insurgent crew from the *Ochakov, Sinop, Chesma, Rostislav* and other vessels plus another 1,515 from the shore-based units were arrested.

TERETS. A 1,200-ton torpedo gunboat built in 1887.

Third Part

Chapter 1 (page 59)
The 'Last Letter' from Schmidt to Riesberg was written from captivity at Ochakov on Christmas Eve 1905. The fourth line echoes John 15:13.

Chapter 2 (page 61)
ROMNY. A town on the railway between Gomel in Byelorussia and Poltava in the Ukraine.

OCHAKOV. A town and naval base sited on a headland on the right bank of the Dnieper esturary some 180 kilometres west of Kherson.

Chapter 4 (page69)
TKACHENKO. A hotel in Ochakov.

Chapter 5 (page 71)
SUB-ESAUL. A Cossack junior captain.

Chapter 6 (page 75)
BEREZAN. A small uninhabited island lying 15 kilometres west of Ochakov.

Chapter 7 (page 79)
SHAROVARY. A type of baggy trousers traditionally worn by Tartars.

NERCHINSK. A penal settlement 300 kilometres east of Chita in East Siberia.

Chapter 8 (page 81)
The trial of Schmidt and his comrades opened on February 7 1906 and lasted a week and a half. The sentences, under Articles 100 and 109 of the Imperial Penal Code for 'armed uprising with the object of overthrowing the state and social system of Russia', were upheld by Vice-Admiral Chukhnin on March 4.

Schmidt's speech has been taken very closely by Pasternak from the court record. Though earlier censored the stanzas omitted have been restored.

KINBURN. A small fortified naval base across the Dnieper estuary from Ochakov.

TARKANKHUT. A peninsular in north-west Crimea some 150 kilometres south-west of Ochakov.

OLVIA. The ancient Greek colony founded by settlers from Miletus in Asia Minor on the site of present-day Ochakov.

Chapter 9 (page 89)
The other three leaders of the mutiny sentenced to the firing squad at Berezan on March 5 were the Bolsheviks, Nikita Antonenko, Sergei Chastnik and Alexander Gladkov. Some further 400 mutineers, including the author, Karnaukhov-Krasukhov, were sent to varying terms of hard labour.

BIBLIOGRAPHY

The original chapters of 'Lieutenant Schmidt' were first published as follows:

First Part: *Novy Mir* 1926, Nos 8-9
Second Part: Chapter 1, *Novy Mir* 1927, Nos 2-4
　　　　　Chapter 2, *Novy Lef* 1927 No 1; *Novy Mir* 1927 No 1
　　　　　Chapter 3, *Novy Mir* 1927 No 3
　　　　　Chapter 4-10: *Novy Mir* 1927, No 4
Third Part: *Novy Mir* 1927, No 5

After extensive cuts whose location is indicated in the preceding notes, 'Lieutenant Schmidt' appeared in its definitive form in 1927 in a combined volume with 'The Year Nineteen-Five'.

Pasternak's son, Evgeny, has produced a documentary account of his father's life and work under the title *Boris Pasternak: Materialy dlya biografii* (Moscow, 1989) of which the second half covering the years 1930 to 1960 has so far appeared in English, entitled *Boris Pasternak The Tragic Years,* (London 1990). Of the various historical sources which Pasternak drew on, the monographs on Schmidt by Karnaukhov-Kraukhov, Voronitsyn and Genkin are accessible in the British Library, while a general account and analysis of the Sevastopol Rising appears as Chapter 18 ('The Red Fleet') of Leon Trotsky's *1905.*

The intensive correspondence conducted between Pasternak, Tsvetaeva and Rilke during the summer of 1926, published under the title *Letters Summer 1926* (London, 1986) provides a moving insight into the author's personality at the time he was writing 'Lieutenant Schmidt'.

The most positive and perceptive of recent critical surveys of 'Lieutenant Schmidt' are to be found in the studies by Peter Levi (*Boris Pasternak,* London 1990), Henry Gifford (*Pasternak,* Cambridge 1977), and Christopher Barnes (*Boris Pasternak: a literary biography,* vol. 1, Cambridge, 1990).

The associated epic, 'The Year Nineteen-Five', translated also by Richard Chappell, is available in the same format and imprint as this edition (London 1989).

VERSE-FORMS

Pasternak cast 'Lieutenant Schmidt' in a wide range of prosodic structures embodying contrasting metres and rhyme-patterns thereby enhancing shifts in mood and tempo, distancing the poet's presence and giving a greater sweep to the narrative. The iambs, trochees, amphibrachs, anapaests and dactyls in lines of one to seven feet have, along with the respective rhyme-patterns, been largely preserved by the English translation in order to recreate the overall impact of the words.